A BOOK BY TALK2DOT

SILENT
WATCHERS

DOT IKWERREGIRL ACHERU

SILENT WATCHERS

Published by Talk2Dot Address www.Talk2Dot.com

(Self Published by Talk2Dot)

This narrative is a true life story. Characters, events and location are factual and are easily verifiable by witnesses and all who walked with me.

ISBN (Hardcover): 978-1-7391666-2-5

ISBN (Paperback): 978-1-7391666-3-2

© 2022 Talk2Dot The Author: Dot IkwerreGirl Acheru Editor: Asari Adeoye Cover design: Sidra _ Lemonade Studios Published and Printed in the United Kingdom First edition 2022

Email: talk2dott@gmail.com Website: www.talk2dot.com

CONTENTS

DEDICATION

Here is a salute to all the mothers, both past and present, continuously counselled to stay in abusive relationships with children as baits, but were bold enough to shun societal pressures as they surged against the norm by walking away, thus gifting a normal life to their children.

This book is also dedicated to all the children that witnessed domestic violence and became resolute to survive, to heal, and to restore, using their experiences as tools to recreate better versions of themselves.

AUTHOR'S NOTE

If I were to pass on one key thing to others it would be that you can be and achieve whatever you want regardless of your situation and in fact against all odds. Furthermore, your peace of mind is paramount...do not compromise it for anything.

We all have a story...OWN IT, SHARE! You are not alone and we are definitely stronger together.

WARNING

THIS BOOK IS NOT SUITABLE FOR READERS UNDER 18 YEARS OF AGE: IT CONTAINS ELEMENTS OF VIOLENCE, SEXUAL CONTENT AND SEXUAL ABUSE.

ACKNOWLEDGMENT

It was not such a feat for me to write a book, what was difficult was the kind of book I was writing. Every word made me relive a traumatic experience which led me back to the words, thoughts and experiences that my subconscious had chosen to bury.

It was a herculean task but the reward was more than I could have ever imagined. All of this would not have been possible without close friends and comrades; Ufuoma Aaron who was constantly rooting for me and pushing me to complete this book. Much thanks to Annet Mugaga MBA, M.A, my friend from University days, who made time to read through my drafts; her impeccable help, keen insight, and ongoing support, has brought my stories to life. She has been a constant support through every struggle and all my successes. This is true friendship.

Writing a book about the story of one's life is a surreal process and so I appreciate my friend Dr. Edem Onofeghara for critically reading through my manuscript and proposing amendments. Additionally, I would like to express gratitude to my editor, Asari Adeoye.

Most importantly, I would like to thank me for believing in me and for doing all this back breaking work. I appreciate myself for not quitting on myself or my children and successfully running 100 hours of activities daily within 24hours. I am grateful to my mother for instilling in me the nature to do more right than wrong. I cannot thank my children enough, my little soldiers, for their support and for choosing this amazing title **Silent Watchers** which encapsulates their part of the story.

To all my fans on social media, too numerous to mention, you guys rock!

INTRODUCTION

F irst off, thank you for buying this book and deciding to read it. Please note that the contents of this book are very explicit but be brave to read this text with the sole aim of learning, arming yourself with necessary information and instruction.

We all heard about a famous woman who publicly and chancily spoke up about her negative life experiences; we subconsciously extract ourselves from such situations and subtly tag these women as 'fiery, aggressive, and foul-mouthed' simply because they stepped out to share their stories of abuse. We might see these boisterous advocates and feel their message is too messy and raw to relate. But being brashly vocal, they make us apprehensive in their cocksure, so we stay silent to avoid becoming one of 'them'.

As a standard, 'nice girls' do not create chaos, they are expected to make lemonade out of lemons, to take their life circumstances as it comes and faithfully believe that these mishaps are ultimately churning out some good from them! *'Nice girls'* neither report cases of sexual harassments or assault from their bosses, nor do they go to the local police when these misdeeds are from their pastors. No! These girls clean themselves up and go on with their lives in denial, like nothing terrible happened and they seek the comfort of others by being mute about their bitter stories and most times hide the pain. Speaking up about abuse requires these *nice girls* to go against what has been inputted in us since childhood – *"Be nice to everyone and do not complain about how others are treating you. Nice girls do not speak up."*

Well, I am not a *nice girl;* daily I tell my story in every possible way with the hopes that someone will wake up and walk out of an abusive relationship. I owned my story, and you should own yours too. Your voice is your power and when we speak up, we identify ourselves and become allies because we are stronger together. I tell my story with pride; while some think my story should stay hidden, some are ashamed on my behalf or think I should be ashamed. Yet, I exude the strength of a woman, a mother, who survived the treacherous perpetrator and escaped with Two wonderful children. My children are my battery source, our story is a path we had to cross, and I hope my journey can be someone's survival guide.

I often look back and say, *"Why was I not told, how did I go unnoticed, why didn't anyone step up and rescue me through all those painful years? How did videos and related materials online elude me?"* The truth is that there are a lot of materials on domestic violence but not enough which is why we still have a huge community of people that are clueless about the topic.

When I share on domestic violence, I take no hostages because I do not want anyone or their children to experience any of the things I had to live through. I will continuously shout about it; being the voice of many voiceless men, women and children out there.

This book is an expose of the disregarded damages of domestic violence on children whom I have dubbed, for the purpose of this book, the "**Silent Watchers.**"

Chapter 1

PURPOSE OF THIS BOOK

T his book serves both as a manifesto and a helpful guide to readers, it is based on a true life story, and its high rating in explicit sexual violence and trigger warnings makes it unsuitable for children.

With a clear aim of inspiring those working with victims of domestic violence, their children and the society that witness domestic violence, this body of work will goad reflections and improvements on how these events are managed while simultaneously revealing what really goes on behind closed doors.

It is informative. On life's path we all learn, we establish what suits our needs, we pick up tricks and hacks for survival and my earnest desire is that you will pick up a few to add to your list as you read this informative material in your hands; but do not be limited in acquiring knowledge; so I advise that you seek further counsel and professional health treatment as this book does not in any way replace the help you can get from a specialist.

It is my hope that many will be roused after reading my story and save themselves and their children from the traumatic paths I ignorantly towed.

In the words of my favourite music artiste of blessed memory,

"I believe the children are our future,

Teach them well and let them lead the way,

Show them all the beauty they possess inside,

Give them a sense of pride to make it easier,

Let the children's laughter remind us how we used to be."

_Greatest Love by **Whitney Houston**

IGNORANCE ISN'T BLISS

Contrary to popular opinions about abusive people or abusive relationships, accepting that you are in an abusive relationship doesn't come easy. After victims are wooed into a relationship with excessive show of love, it is difficult to comprehend why that perfect person changes.

As far as I know, I was once in an abusive relationship. My nearly eight-year marriage was miserable, laborious, terrible and dominating. For the first 7 years, I did not realise I was in an abusive relationship, let alone call it domestic violence. One particular reason, same like for many others before me, was that I did not fit my own preconceptions of a victim of abuse. I was the breadwinner in my relationship, a successful, confident career woman, a good Christian and considered myself on the average, a good judge of character. I had traveled the world on my own, lived overseas for years and I did not have a history of abusive relationships, neither did I have daddy issues. My personal experience taught me that you could be all I have listed above and yet fall prey to abuse; without the right exposure or knowledge of domestic violence you can still fall headlong into a relationship with a controlling, manipulating, vindictive and abusive person who is very clever at hiding their alter-ego behind a veil of charm when they first meet you. Remember that abusers are master manipulators and they have indeed had years of practice before they met you. I assumed my situation was more about a person with temper and anger issues, alongside, low self-esteem, and I did not realise that domestic violence was beyond physical violence.

Abusers can appear to be quite "normal" when you first meet them. But during your relationship they push puny, microscopic and undetected steps further towards abuse; red flags as we call them. The downside is if you are absolutely oblivious of what those red flags are. Another thing is that they speed up a relationship so that they can hide their true nature long enough to get you hooked. Basically people can hide their true character for up to six months, so just like that, without realising it, you are living in a relationship you'd never willingly chose.

After I came out of my abusive marriage, I realised that it was not just me; it had become commonplace daily. It was happening to the smartest and the toughest, not just the stereotypes. So many people in my circle were going through or had gone through similar or worse. Coming to the consciousness that many supposedly perfect marriages were not as wonderful as they'd been trying to portray in self-deceit and that they were in abusive relationships. Just like them, I hid it quite well.

I cannot over emphasize the fact that domestic violence or domestic abuse (used interchangeably) can happen to anyone, regardless of age, social background, gender, religion, sexuality or ethnicity. Whilst domestic violence happens in all kinds of relationships (heterosexual, lesbian, gay, bisexual and transgender), tons of resources and statistics online have proved that the vast majority of domestic violence incidents are carried out by men and experienced by women.

The kind of abuse a person experiences can be physical, emotional, psychological, financial or sexual as the case may be. In my case hmm... I pretty much experienced all of these at different stages of my marriage. Let me break it down to simple understandable points; if, for instance, you or anyone is ever forced to alter their behaviour because they are frightened of their partner's reaction, that person is being abused. Heck! I wish someone had told me this. Abuse can begin at any stage of the relationship and as such domestic violence is rarely a one-off. Incidents generally become more frequent and severe over a period of time.

When I finally broke free of the shackles of an abusive marriage, I decided to actively talk about my situation with the hopes that someone out there would wake up and save themselves or save someone else from this tragedy. I could never really understand why no one spotted what I was going through or spoke up about it, but now I realise that just like me, a lot of people were and still are clueless about domestic violence and how to handle it.

Domestic violence is a critical issue; and I would like to highlight some of the signs of an abusive relationship. It could be very tough to decipher and like I said, I was in it for seven ignorant years. For some others, denial might be their coping mechanism, believing that indeed their partners aren't abusive.

In my seventh year of marriage, I met someone; she was the one that literally revived me. We all need that one person to do that for us. She had visited my family, invited by the ex-husband to settle a feud. What she witnessed was the beginning of my redemption. She was the first person to mention Domestic violence, and not only that, she gave real life examples that were exactly what I was going through. Heck! *"How did I, the all-knowing, all so smart, exposed intelligent Dot not know this"*, I thought. I had actually managed a Project on Domestic violence and re-offenders, but I never saw myself as one of the victims. *"What in the voodoo name am I dealing with here?"* Anyways, she bumped it up a notch by saying, *"Go and read up about domestic violence, with a focus on emotional and psychological abuse"*

For the past three years, I have actively advocated against domestic violence because I took a cue from this lady, which leads me to ...

- Explain to people the true nature of domestic violence and highlight the *non-violent* aspect, as this is where a lot of people fail to realise its existence.

- Give real life examples because it always helps to have something to relate it to. I always say, *"Once you see one abusive relationship, you probably seen them all."* So the examples will always hit home hard.

- Encourage victims to research on the topic. Trust me, this is always the breaking point. Once you start Googling, it's like an endless cesspit of stories and most of those stories are the same stories for every victim, and this serves as *'the wakeup'* call.

In my case, number 3 was the definite wakeup call so to speak. So I began to look up things online about my relationship, starting with the one thing I thought might be the problem in my home- Jealousy. This birthed control, toxic communication and finally domestic violence. All of these were very new concepts to me but the more I researched, the more I was shocked and appalled at what I had been subjected to, foolishly believing that these things could change or get better. Possibly, in the course of reading this book, if you are experiencing any of the things mentioned then you need to take immediate action because it doesn't get better for anyone, it didn't for me. So know that you cannot change these perpetrators, change can only come when a person realises they need to change and seeks personal help.

As improbable as it may seem, many people do not know they are in an abusive relationship. Most people are pretty much aware of physical violence and that is what they look out for and tell themselves they will never tolerate a partner that hits them. Another myth is that abusive people are monsters 24/7, they look like monsters and you can identify them once you see them. Contrary to that, emotional, psychological and mental abuse are usually overlooked and considered a norm in a few societies. They are not seen as domestic violence because there are no discernible signs of physical violence associated with it.

I always say, if you do not understand a language and all of the answers you seek are spoken via that same language, the required information is futile! More so, without knowledge of the traits to watch for, you would not recognise domestic violence even if it came up and smacked you right in the face! Can a person be in an abusive relationship and not know? Absolutely! Numerous people have found themselves in abusive relationships and do not realise it until they are well into the relationship. I happily use myself as an example because this abusive scenario does not play out premised on societal background, which is why recently at a conference, I started by listing my achievements and then said, I am also a survivor of domestic violence and yup! The room became graveyard silent.

I found myself in this very plight with an abusive partner, and it took me well over seven years to understand what I was up against at the time; it felt like there were no solutions or answers. My abusive partner counted on the fact that I was family orientated, hated failure, disliked confrontation, thought about the children and the impacts of a broken home, and knew he had latched on and caged the perfect victim. Like most people, at the time, if you said *"abuse"* or *"Domestic Violence"*, my thoughts would immediately point to physical violence. I did not imagine or consider other types of abuse like financial abuse, emotional abuse, coercion and control, or sexual abuse. Let me digress a little about sexual abuse.

People think about only the violent type of this abuse and also excuse everything done in marriage. Sexual abuse includes rape (violent and non-violent) and withholding of sex, as well as marital rape which is another topic which lacks popular discourse. I also did not consider other personality types like psychopaths, narcissists or sociopaths to mention a few. I never realised that what I was living with was potentially undiagnosed mental health; it was after I left I began to hear words like, Bipolar, Schizophrenia, split and multiple personality, fully blown psychosis. I was not to blame, I had never seen a *'high functioning'* mental health patient. In Nigeria, my country of origin, "mad" people as we call them, usually roam the streets naked with nappy hair. So until it gets to that stage, we never really take it seriously.

A couple of people and I share this problem, we lived a certain way, interacted with certain kinds of people and were pretty much sheltered from the weird realities of life up until marriage. And while I felt I was well exposed, well educated, well-traveled, I did not realise that in my whole life, I had not garnered any skills or strategies to even avoid this type of person, I did not know people like these existed, and had never met anyone like that let alone how to get out of it. It was like something out of a movie to say the least.

I want to reassure victims of abuse, survivors of abuse and those merely seeking knowledge on the topic that, being unaware of abuse is normal, especially in the early stages. Abuse has to be tolerated in order to persist then mature, and because of the lack of physical expressions in some cases, people do not realise they are being abused and so they tolerate it. After all, *"No one is perfect"*, *"People can change"*, *"He said he was sorry"*, *"He brought me roses"*, *"My case is not the worst"*, *"Others have had it worse than me"* along with other self-denial clichés; while some ignorantly tolerate abuse because they do not feel like they have a choice or they actually *do not* have a choice. Some victims live in denial and others are conditioned to believe that they are to blame for the problems.

9

People never really know how dangerous and destructive the impact of domestic abuse can be on the victims. A common question or thought is, *"If it's as bad as they say, why don't they leave?"* People on the outside looking in often do not grasp just how serious it can be. It's never as easy as just standing up for yourself or just leaving because the abusers often have had such a hold on their victim that everything the victim does is to appease their abuser, because it'll make it a little bearable or every word uttered is turned into ammunition that'll be used against the victims. Once you step back and view the big picture, it will register that you are in an abusive relationship, you can then analyze and compare it to other abusive relationships, and this awakening gives a clearer picture of why victims do not leave. The Eureka moment, when you concede *"I'm one of them!"* often marks the end of the relationship as they finally see it for what it is. This epiphany occurs when victims have watched others stay in abusive relationships.

ABOUT DOMESTIC VIOLENCE

Domestic violence also called Domestic abuse or Intimate Partner Violence is primarily about control. It is a pattern of behaviour in any relationship that is employed to gain or maintain power and control over an intimate partner. Abuse is any physical, sexual, emotional, economic or psychological actions or threats of actions that negatively influence another person. This includes any behaviours that frighten, intimidate, terrorise, manipulate, hurt, humiliate, blame or injure someone. I must reiterate that domestic abuse can happen to anyone of any race, age, sexual orientation, religion, or gender. It can occur within a range of relationships including couples who are married, living together or dating. Domestic violence affects people of all socioeconomic backgrounds and education levels. Domestic abuse is typically manifested as a pattern of abusive behaviour toward an intimate partner in a dating or family relationship, where the abuser exerts unnecessarily powerful control over the victim. Incidents are rarely isolated, and usually escalate in frequency and severity. Domestic abuse may culminate in serious physical injury or eventual death.

THE LITMUS TEST

I bet you are asking yourself, *"So how do I know if I am being emotionally abused?"* Here's a quick test, ask yourself these questions as they really helped me acknowledge a few things about my situation. Does your partner or former partner ever...

- Belittle you or put you down?
- Isolate you from your family and friends?
- Stop you going to college or work?
- Make unreasonable demands for your attention?
- Accuse you of flirting or having affairs?
- Tell you what to wear, who to see, where to go, and what to think?

- Control your money or not give you enough to buy food or other essential things?

In the first section, sadly, I answered yes to all. Surprisingly I was still hoping I was wrong. If you have responded positively to a few of the above, then you are definitely being emotionally abused. But just like me, you may think you can manage it; after all, you have managed this situation for a few years. What you do not know or realise is how much psychological, emotional and physical damage is taking place inside you.

The next thing you need to know is the bit no one wants to ever imagine about the love of their life - How dangerous could this person be or are they even dangerous. Another way to ascertain abuse is the existence of threats of violence and intimidation. Note that at this point it is just threats and not actual physical violence. Ask yourself again, does your partner or former partner, ever:

- Threaten to hurt or kill you?
- Destroy things that belong to you?
- Stand over you, invade your personal space?
- Threaten to kill themselves or the children?
- Read your emails, texts or letters?
- Harass or follow you?

In this section, I scored five out of six and this is where fear literally kicked in. I had been sitting on a ticking time bomb and did not realise it. Every single thing I read or consulted screamed **RUN!** If you are like me, I would urge you to consider doing the same, but there's a process and so this needs to be approached with absolute caution.

Let's talk about the most popular bit in domestic violence, Physical abuse. The person abusing you may hurt you in a number of ways, and so does your partner or former partner, ever...

- Slap, hit or punch you?
- Push or shove you?
- Bite or kick you?
- Burn you?
- Choke you or hold you down?
- Throw things?

In this bit I scored three out of six. However, I can assure you that once you wake up and refuse to be abused then more physical violence will kick in. If they cannot control you psychologically and emotionally, they will hit you to make you remember that you have to stay in line. This was exactly my case. As usual, I tell people, **DON'T WAIT TO GET HIT.**

Another area that most people tread carefully on is Sexual abuse especially within the confines of 'marriage'. It is assumed that this doesn't happen in marriage because once you are married your bodies belong to each other. Spousal rape is something you dare not mention, in fact it is a taboo, and I mean, how you can even imagine that? You will be told this like I was, *"How can I rape my OWN wife."* Information and awareness is everything, and once you are alert, trust me, you may feel a bit vile and contaminated but you will be alright.

Sexual abuse can happen to anyone, whether they are male or female. To examine the true state of things in that department, ask yourself, does your partner or former partner ever,

- Touch you in a way you do not want to be touched?

- Make unwanted sexual demands?

- Hurt you during sex?

- Pressure you to have unsafe sex – for example, not using a condom?

- Pressure you to have sex?

- Demand expression of his/her sexual fantasies?

If your partner, or former partner, has sex with you when you do not want to, this is rape. Surprisingly, in this section I scored six out of six. Your body is your body and your choices should be respected. Coercion and control is one of the new laws in the United Kingdom from a few years ago. Sadly, it is one grey area quite difficult to convict a perpetrator. Remember that these abusers are pretty sneaky and will say anything to snake their way out of a situation.

Ask yourself again,

- Have you ever felt afraid of your partner or former partner?

- Have you ever changed your behaviour because you are afraid of what your partner, or former partner, might do?

This was a clear two out of two. I do not know what your scores are so far but if you have read this far, you are either going through abuse or know a few people who are. So how can you help someone who is being abused? If you are worried a friend is being abused, let them know you have noticed something is amiss. They might not be ready to talk, but try to find quiet times when they can speak, if they choose to. And if someone confides in you that they're suffering domestic abuse:

1. Listen and take care not to blame them.

2. Acknowledge that it takes strength to talk to someone about experiencing abuse.

3. Make time to talk, but do not push them to speak if they are unwilling to admit the reality of their frightening and challenging situation. Tell them nobody deserves to be threatened or beaten, regardless of what the abuser has said.

4. Please do not ask them to stay or endure even if they do not mention physical violence; abuse is abuse; irrespective of the type... nobody deserves to be treated that way.

5. Most victims may not admit to domestic violence so you can throw it in that nobody deserves to live in an unhappy place.

What else can you do to help? Support them as a friend, encourage them to express their feelings, and allow them to make their own decisions. Sometimes you may have to help them make that decision because they are probably disoriented, depressed, got PTSD and /or Complex PTSD and will not be in the right state of mind to decide. So you will need to give them practical steps and if you are unsure of steps to take in assisting them, please consult agencies that manage such situations. You can also make an anonymous call to the police.

If they have suffered physical harm, offer to go with them to a hospital or help them report the assault to the police if they choose to. Most importantly, be ready to provide information on organisations.

If you are unable to do much about the situation and you are worried that a friend, neighbour or loved one is a victim of domestic abuse then you can call the National Domestic Abuse Helpline for free and confidential advice. It is open 24 hours a day on 0808 2000 247 for those in the United Kingdom. For other locations, do try to find out organisations that deal with domestic violence issues. If you believe there is an immediate risk of harm to someone, or if it is an emergency, you should always call 999 or the emergency number of your country of abode.

THE OTHERS...

Now that we have established what domestic violence is in summary and what victims and perpetrators may look like, let us talk about the other victims of abuse.

Do you know that victims of domestic abuse may also include a child or other relative, or any other cohabitant of your home? As much as I would love to talk about my nearly eight years of trauma, my main focus in this book; **Silent Watchers**, are the children! If I had a penny for every time I heard a woman say I am staying for my children, or a woman was advised to stay for her children, I would be rich.

Just like many women, I stayed a while for my children, I had to, there was no option or so I thought but once I was awakened to the truth of domestic violence, I plotted my escape and ran without looking back. In fact, if I knew back then what I know now, I should have left earlier than I did. And this is why I need every victim of abuse; men and women to listen to my story, the story that was hidden... the story of the S**ilent Watchers**.

Chapter 2

SILENT WATCHERS

W henever I talk about children and marriages or relationships, I always insist that, *"Children do best in a safe loving environment, whether with one parent or with two."* I say this because there is too much negativity attached to children from broken homes, and this is why many people stay in toxic relationships because they feel the children need both parents under one roof, or that a single parent, especially mothers, is a recipe for a wrecked child. But what most people forget is that some homes are already destroyed, and in turn are destroying the child. Some parents may actually be better parents to their kids if they were not already struggling to deal with a toxic partner

Funnily enough, parents also think they can hide unhappiness, tears and abuse from their children. Children are silent watchers and you will be surprised at how much they know. They can feel your pain, your emotions, whether happy or sad. Never underestimate them and the positive impact of nurturing them in a safe space versus an unsafe place. I always admit my limitation in knowledge, yet there is a lot I have learned, and there is a lot I am still learning and unlearning. As much as people praised and still praise me as the super mum that rescued and saved her kids, as I studied the impact of domestic abuse on children, sincerely I wept and still do so frequently. You see, ignorance is not an excuse, ignorance will not give you a free pass in life, and rather ignorance will punish you and put you in very vulnerable places.

The things I lived through and experienced were like the stuff I watched on TV, Criminal and psychological programs. I could never have imagined it. These things are never taught in churches. Yup, I had to drag the church in here. Now out there in the world, people are a whole lot more "woke" and would handle domestic abuse in a different way, while the church will ask you to pray, or shout *"It is not my portion"* Ha! The impact of domestic abuse on children is nothing less than traumatic, and should be avoided by all means; if you can't think about saving yourself, please save your children. Children growing up in abusive homes are negatively impacted emotionally; they may either become overly sensitive, or completely numb. The social and cognitive effects of being in such an environment are more severe and long-lasting than could be imagined. Such children will either be aggressive and lash out at the slightest provocation or become completely withdrawn and submissive. It also makes a child feel helpless, afraid, and enraged due to feelings of injustice and powerlessness. These children in adulthood may have conflicts with authority, people and have a deficit in anger management. They could also turn their aggression on themselves or others and become aggressive, passive, or passive-aggressive.

Furthermore, children who are exposed to abuse and trauma may develop PTSD, anxiety and incur the inability to cope with stress. They may also become unable to regulate their emotions, have sleep disorders, lower immunity and potential physical illness leading up to adulthood. Like I said earlier on, remaining in that abusive situation with kids as an excuse will ultimately destroy them now and their future; physically, mentally and emotionally and the list is endless. You should be leaving for your children!

On the one hand, boys will react to domestic abuse as stated above, while on the other hand girls are more likely to internalise their distress. Girls could turn out to be withdrawn from other people, and they may experience anxiety and depression from a young age. As they grow up they may have an inferiority complex and complain of vague physical symptoms. They are more likely to have an eating disorder, or to harm themselves by taking overdoses or cutting themselves up. These children may experience one or all of these; anxiety, depression, trouble learning, trouble paying attention, memory problems, problems with self-control, and low self-esteem.

So are you still thinking of staying in that toxic place for the sake of your children? Are you still telling others to do the same? Do you think these children do not impact you in your perfectly groomed family? I am smirking as I write this; remember that, we all exist in the space, world, same earth, so one way or the other, these children from abusive homes will meet others from non-abusive homes either in school, workplace environment, or in relationships and potentially that cycle of abuse will continue. So while you may think it doesn't directly affect you, it does. It is our civil duty to step in when we see ongoing abuse. I mean look at it from this perspective, if you saw a child on fire, or being raped wouldn't you go to save them? Well, that is how seriously we need to take these issues. Domestic violence is not just a crime to humanity, it is a crime against humanity.

Before I progress, if you are really thinking about your children, and this message is for the *"sane"* member of the relationship not the abuser (as you know, abusers do not think they are wrong and will justify their actions. Besides they really do not feel the pain of others, they are selfish and self-centred; NARCISSISTS), I need you to think about these potential lifelong damages to your lovely child or children as the case may be. Think about potential mental health disorders such as anxiety, attachment issues, and post-traumatic stress and depression disorders, self-harming or suicidal thoughts, learning disorders, including poor language and cognitive development, developmental delay, eating disorders and physical ailments. Think about how abuse affects you as an adult and then how it affects your child. The mental war you are consistently fighting is the same war they are fighting as well; sadly their little brains are not fully formed at that stage in life so the impact is grave.

Some of the other things I never knew was that research has found that emotional abuse is linked to thinning of certain areas of the brain that help you manage emotions and be self-aware.... hmmm.... Thinking back about my son... now it makes sense. You see, I could never really understand my son between the ages of 12 months to 5 years. He seemed to have no control over his emotions. In fact I doubt that he understood what emotions were and how and when to use them. It was quite difficult to understand when he would have an outburst or just be happy. My daughter would scream for just no reason. For instance, I would announce *"mealtime"* and a child just starts crying uncontrollably. My son at just over a year old would get angry over the slightest thing, and punch the flat screen TV so hard that you would see white flashes on the screen, coupled with slamming doors, smashing my mobile phone. If he was watching a kids program on the phone and a YouTube Ad came up, he would scream and throw the phone on the wall so hard that it would split open; batteries out, SIM the opposite direction and I thought it was too much rage inside for a child that young. I also thought he was picking that up from his dad; I never connected to the trauma of witnessing emotional abuse. On the flip side, he could just sit and laugh uncontrollably for no reason and hey, let us not forget that sometimes he would just go quiet mode for no apparent reason.

Domestic violence is notoriously known for its ability to lead to epigenetic or genetic change and ultimately depression for a child experiencing and or witnessing domestic violence. The consternations of abuse are apparent in primary victims; children who witness the abuse of their mothers, fathers, or other family members, are also impacted. I call domestic violence a pandemic which a lot of people are treating with levity, it is not getting the deserved attention and publicity it should. For instance, in the United Kingdom, the police recorded a total of 1,459,663 domestic abuse-related incidents and crimes in England and Wales in the year ending March 2021. Out of these, 845,734 were recorded as domestic abuse-related crimes, an increase of 6% from the previous year, representing 18% of all offences recorded by the police in the year ending March 2021. Estimates from the most recent Crime Survey for England and Wales year ending March 2020 show 5.5% of adults aged 16 to 74 years (2.3 million) experienced domestic abuse in the 12 months prior. (Source: CSEW) Now imagine how many children are witnessing or have witnessed domestic violence, also imagine how many children will grow up with mental disorders, epigenetic changes, anxiety, depression and most of all grow to continue the cycle of abuse by becoming abusers themselves. This is the United Kingdom where there is a little bit of law and order, imagine places like Africa, Asia and other developing countries where domestic abuse is almost a norm?

Important self-examination questions would bo,

- Do I want to create a mentally dysfunctional child?

- Do I want my boy child to grow up to become a potentially abusive husband and dad?

- Do I want my girl child to grow up to become abusive, numb to her emotions and /or end up in an abusive relationship because that is what she saw growing up?"

If your answers are in the negative to any of these, you are on the right track, but the weightier question is, *what are you going to do about it?*

Never forget that research has proved that these victims of abuse, children who witnessed abuse, may become abuse themselves and in fact they are usually completely unaware that they have switched roles so deeply; they see themselves as victimized, disempowered, small, abandoned and unloved. You may not see these signs now and think its ok but take note that there is a lot of research out there that proves that when the time comes and your kids get in a relationship or get married, the pattern begins to emerge and their parents' destinies are repeated.

Boys often grow up to be men who will succumb to the urge to abuse their wives physically or emotionally while girls will become battered wives themselves, rationalizing how their marriages are different from those of their mothers, even though the similarity is uncanny. Aggression is seen as a valid way of dealing with frustration. It is intertwined with love and marriage, forming a cancerous web of cyclic abuse and affection that leaves no one unharmed. So do not say I never told you.

MY STORY CONTINUES...

Sometimes I crossed troubled waters. I was unacquainted with the generational damage, yet one thing I knew was that I did not want to raise a violent son, a son that would disrespect me, or treat women like trash. I had witnessed my ex talk down and shout at his mother and his elder sisters. As for his brother, he had absolutely no regard for him. I really could not imagine having a son do that to me. I also did not want to raise a daughter that became like me who allowed herself to be treated unjustly, after all I thought, *"I was the only real life example of what a mother and a wife should be... be quiet and do everything to keep the peace, even if it required giving up yourself."* NEVER! I just wanted them to have a "normal" and fair upbringing. I wanted them to have a peaceful home and learn how dialogue could answer most things, how boundaries should be respected, and how rage and uncontrollable temper was not an option. Little did I know that I was dealing with a lot more than anticipated. Looking back, I'm glad I broke out and yes, perhaps I did save my little ones. Hey! I have to give myself some props from time to time.

It cannot be over emphasized that the effects of domestic abuse on children may be apparent within a short period of time, while other grievous damages may be noticed in tho long run, so please think about your children's future. Using my children as classic examples, they were usually on edge; their behaviours were unpredictable at home and in public. Whenever the abusive ex began his two hours of rage in a circular endless conversation, the kids would begin to scream, slam toys or sometimes just be quiet and watch. Screaming and slamming toys were their *method of coping,* sometimes it actually got me off the hook because the abuser could not cope with the noise and walked away. Over a period of time of constantly witnessing abuse, the children seemed to live in bated breath, in anticipation of the subsequent verbal assault. About the age of two years, my son would wet himself whenever his dad began those "sessions" and sometimes even craps himself. I also noticed that their behaviours were different and somewhat calm in the absence of the abuser but once he arrived, the kids would scream for no reason, bang toys and ignore him. These behaviours naturally conferred more abuse on me as I was blamed for brainwashing a two year old at one point... like seriously? He actually said,

"You have connived with this boy to wet himself or to poop on himself whenever I am talking, just so I won't make my point." and other times, blamed me for not teaching the kids to love their dad.

"Children should come to welcome their dad, however when I get home it seems i never returned, they just act like I don't exist." he said.

I remember once interjecting, *"...but maybe they are scared of you?"* Another time, I said, *"Maybe you should make more efforts to getting to know your kids and spending more time with them"*

Obviously both occasions blessed me with a mouthful of insults. To me it was not just about the insults, but about how loudly he shouted and more importantly him doing this in the presence of the kids. I remember always advising myself that I needed to calm him down no matter the cost; I cannot have these kids listen to this. Sometimes I pleaded that I put the kids in another bedroom but no, he had to ridicule me in front of them. Thus, in his absence, I would look my son eyeball to eyeball and say,

"You will never disrespect me or any woman like this, and you will be a gentleman and treat people right." And to my daughter I would then say, *"I am weak but you do not have to be like me, I see the fire in your eyes, do not ever let no one quench it. Never be disrespected by anyone, not even me."*

My kids would just stare at me clueless, but I did it anyways, and all the time that I had them with me in his absence.

NIGHT DRAMA

Let's talk about night-time in my home. It was nothing short of a nightmare for me, talk about increased crying and whining for no apparent reason. My kids would stay up until way past midnight. I would have to lay down on their bed, singing, reading and doing all sorts to calm them. Finally just after midnight, they would give into sleep and be up again at 4am. I never imagined that some of these behaviours may have been a result of them witnessing abuse. Some children will actually regress. I remember how my son got to three and half years, and would not walk, talk, or feed himself any longer. Like all the things he had been doing just stopped. I wondered how that could be. At the time, the health visitor put it down to attention seeking since his sister was just about 6 months old. But now I know and with much studying and research that it isn't uncommon for pre-schoolers who witness domestic violence to revert to the habits of younger children.

For those with older children, school-aged children could develop anti-social traits and may struggle with guilt over the abuse witnessed. These children typically take on the blame for the abuse their parent deals with, a belief that can strongly bruise their self-esteem. My son was very anti-social and still struggles with that. In fact it was put down to a social communication disorder. I did not know I was being abused, I knew I was not happy and things were not right, but I never had the opportunity or was too scared to talk about it. Sadly, no one else noticed.

One of the most devastating effects of domestic violence is its capability to cause post-traumatic stress disorder in children that are raised around it. Despite being spared from physical abuse, the trauma of domestic violence is enough to cause dangerous changes in the developing brains of children. Much later my son was diagnosed with ASD, Autism Spectrum Disorder, could our living situation have caused this? These changes to children's brain architecture in their formative years may cause nightmares, changes in sleep patterns, anger, irritability, difficulty concentrating, and children may sometimes have the ability to re-enact aspects of the traumatizing abuse observed. Like earlier mentioned, night time sleep was a problem, but day time sleep was a little bit better though it occurred at awkward hours of the day.

Bear in mind that mental health strains are a common result of witnessing the abuse of a parent and these consequences may sometimes be apparent in their physical well-being. I have read that school-aged children may report headaches and stomach pains which are traceable to the tense situation back home. In infants, there is a higher risk of experiencing physical injury following the constant stream of abuse on a parent. Interestingly, when my son was between the ages of three and five (just before I left the toxic, Chernobyl house), he was almost always sick, coughs, catarrh, throwing up, difficulties in breathing, skin issues, rash, eczema etc. Again I was blamed for not taking care of him properly, from *"maybe your hands were not clean*

when you fed him," to *"maybe you are not feeding him right...*
he should not be interacting with people... you should not let
people touch him... now you see what has happened." I could
never have imagined at the time that my living situation
was causing his poor state of health. As we say in Nigeria,
"had I known." I write this so that some of you who are still
insisting on staying for the children will learn that you
should be leaving that environment for them!

For those with much older children, research has shown
that when teenagers witness domestic abuse, they tend to
act out in reaction to the situation. They may fight, skip
school, engage in risky sexual activities, or dabble in drugs
and alcohol. These teenagers are also very likely to get in
trouble with the law. In many instances, children that live
in abusive households are also likely to fall victim to this
treatment themselves. An abusive partner can very easily
become an abusive parent or guardian; physically, verbally,
and emotionally harming their children.

WITNESS TO DOMESTIC VIOLENCE-LONG TERM EFFECT

Now, I know that just like me you want to secure your sacred
marriage, I mean, what would people say if they found out
your seemingly perfect marriage was a scam for real? HEY!
WAKE UP! Save your children first, and then you can think
about your perfect marital image. Take your children away
from such an environment and then take yourself away too.

Now that you know that domestic violence can have lasting effects on the physical, mental, and later life of children, what are you going to do? It is crucial to adequately shield them from abuse. While I was in my abusive marriage not knowing I was being abused and the impact it may have on my kids, I tried a few things because for me it was all about protecting the kids. I was actually ashamed of my home as I was not raised like that, and in fact the things going on at home were like things I had watched on TV but heck this was real. Whenever the abusive violent sessions started, I would keep calm no matter what. This was a decision I made after I noticed my son started having accidents. For a fact, after years of abuse, I began to believe it was my fault; I deserved it etc, but know this, it is not your fault and you have to remind yourself daily of these facts:

- It is a toxic home.
- You are with an abusive person that will indeed lash out on you for any reason at all.
- No matter what you have done, no one deserves to be emotionally abused, and
- If it is happening to you without your consent, then it's wrong.

HOW TO COPE

In the first few months of marriage, I tried to talk back and argue my opinions to be heard, but I got tired. I pretty much figured out that his desire was to be confrontational, which could easily escalate and be justified. I caged every urge to talk back after my son turned two. It is normal to want to retaliate, yell, or cry when you are being abused but try to stay calm and resist the temptation. Think about your kids watching and never try to assume a personality that isn't you. If you can,

- Get out of the room or take deep breaths, inhale for 6 seconds and then exhale after three seconds.

- Keep reassuring yourself of the positives reasons why ignoring him/her will be the best for you as you also

- Maintain a physical distance, and

- Distract yourself by thinking of something that you enjoy, you can even imagine yourself on the beach.

My safe place was Jamaica, lounging by the seaside, sipping milk from a coconut, while receiving a shoulder and back massage from a Taye Diggs looking fella and *"Everything gonna be alright"* by Bob Marley playing in the background. Create your own your mind space.

These techniques worked for me in my later years when I had realised the relationship was abusive and an unresolvable state. However, in my earlier years, I had to sit there and listen to his rant; he would stop me if I tried to leave the room. I then decided to kneel and pleadingly apologize each time, saying and doing whatever it took to make him stop. It would still take nothing less than 2 hours to calm him, leading to forced sex, where I had to moan, fake an orgasm and acknowledge that it was fine. Hey, if that is what it took to have some peace, then yeah I did it.

Try not to react to abuse, it will later make you feel worse and have a negative impact on your mental health, leaving you disturbed for hours; therefore, make bold to ignore and not answer back. If you are overwhelmed with whatever they have said, you can go into your room and cry, but once you stop, try meditation to control your emotions. If you are not a confrontational person, do not try to be. These abusers thrive on your negative energy.

Don't stay for your kids, leave for them. Leave and give them the opportunity of a normal life. Understand that the negative effects are more on the children than on you.

Chapter 3

PREGNANCY ONE

M ysteriously in the midst of all my hellish experiences in the marriage, from quarrels through the night, screaming and spewing insults (one time the housing agents called complaining that the neighbours had raised concerns) to sleepless nights, forced and repulsive sex. I was not eating well, constantly unhappy and in tears, worn down emotionally, mentally, physically as well as financially and then I got pregnant six months into the marriage. I thought I would have a break from the emotional abuse and threats of violence, I felt like my relief had come. I hoped that this pregnancy would bring about some maturity in the way we went about our conversations and interactions with each other, I hoped he would go easy on me, after all I learnt pregnant women were pampered.

To be honest, I did not know I was pregnant, I just had this very unusual itchy irritation, I think we both did if I recall. This led to a trip to the GP (General Practitioners) and a referral to the sexual health clinic. At the sexual health clinic all tests came out clear, but then there was news about pregnancy. Wow! That was a shocker; we were both happy... so I thought. I remember thinking, things were going to change. There would be less aggravation; I mean everyone knows pregnant women need to be in a good state of mind, during conception-gestation. On the contrary, pregnancy did not get me the free pass I anticipated. My ex-husband and I had not been doing well for the past months, nothing made much sense and he had become increasingly emotionally and verbally abusive. It had been really rough and pregnancy was not going to change a thing. Having sex while pregnant was painfully uncomfortable, really; I was only a few weeks pregnant, and he was going at me like we were a bunch of teenagers exploring ourselves for the first time. I tried to talk about it but it all fell to deaf ears and several times culminated in insults. I was constantly reminded that as a wife, according to the bible, my body belongs to him and I must never reject him just like he had never rejected me. Now the thing with my ex-husband was that he was hyper-sexed, we are talking 40 to 50 minutes of grinding before he would ejaculate, on demand sex two to three times daily even when I was on my period. I lacked sleep, peace and happiness, as much as I loved him, this whole sex thing was becoming an unpleasant chore. With or without consent he would either be rubbing, grinding, squeezing my nipples really tightly, fingers up my coochie; I felt completely violated and numb. Those first weeks of pregnancy brought about painfully sore nipples, but he still would not let go and I just taught myself to stay calm and hoped the baby would be fine. This was supposed to be my reward for marriage, the joy of a new life.

SPOUSAL RAPE AND HEART BREAK

I got used to the fact that my 'no' would be ignored, or would bring about insults which I found embarrassing because while he did not care if the neighbours heard, I did. I would be asleep or trying to sleep when he would come into the room and say *"I need you"* and in my mind I would be like *"Here we go again!"* because even if I refused him, he would keep insisting, saying things like, *"Pregnant women are always horny, what is wrong with you?"* or *"Oh! you say you do not want to but you are still going to start moaning and piss yourself in a few minutes, please relax."* Finally I would just go numb, zone out and let go. I would feel really stupid and feel like I should have done something else, but it was all quite shocking how he carried on regardless of my refusal. With time I got accustomed to it since it was already the norm before pregnancy, I guess I expected differently during pregnancy.

I did not know there was such a thing as spousal rape, in fact non-violent spousal rape. I found out about spousal rape 7 years later and you can only imagine how disgusted and vile I felt. Anyway, sex usually left me sore and he would say, *"...that is because your skin is so soft'*. He had an auto response for every situation. The pressure for sex was unreal especially during the first weeks of pregnancy. Imagine trying to grow a healthy baby in that condition?

Flash forward to a 12 weeks dating scan, we missed the appointment because we were really late for it; he was notorious for being late for everything. He believed he was special and the world would wait for him, he constantly referred to Keanu Reeves in the Matrix. How to bend the spoon by believing there is no spoon, the metaphysics, how to bend and control time. We got to the appointment later and the mid-wife and health professionals had to rebook us in for a few weeks later. Right there at the clinic he kicked off, shouting and raging that they have to see his wife now. Of course the nurse calmly explained to him that we were over 40minutes late and there were no other appointments for the day, and they could not see us when there were others waiting. He continued shouting and the nurse threatened to call the security on us if we did not leave. I held his arm and urged him to let it go. You see things like that usually provoked him further because his expectation was that as a wife I ought to join him in the confrontation. Me? NEVER!

I was unhappy about this because I was keen on seeing a scan, I just wanted some joy. After the appointment, the emotional and sexual abuse continued. It was about the time of the London 2012 Olympics and we went to see the grounds. We bumped into a family we knew from the church we used to attend, the lady was pregnant. She was only 10 weeks pregnant and her belly was way bigger than mine. I began to wonder, is there something wrong with mine? I mentioned it to him that I was a bit worried that my belly did not seem to be growing and I felt like I had no connection with my growing child. He retorted that I was unnecessarily over dramatizing, that everything was fine. Oh well, the spiritual head had spoken. I did have a few weird dreams, which I said made me feel like there was something wrong with the baby, but he shouted at me claiming that I brought bad luck and I needed to renew my mind, and of course we had make up sex and moved on.

It was now time for the appointment at 16 weeks pregnant. We got there and I was so excited, could not wait to see my little one. I had mixed feelings but I remained hopeful. I had never been pregnant, never followed pregnancy gist or pregnant women so I did not know what to expect. As the doctor performed my sonogram, I watched as he held my hands and then I died and woke up when I heard,

"No fetal movement" I really cannot explain how it felt. I knew something was not right but how could anything be right based on how we lived. I asked the doctor, just to be sure what he meant by no fetal movement. He said,

"I'm sorry but there is no movement with your baby, your baby is gone." To say I was broken is an understatement yet I managed to hold back the tears. Why couldn't life just give me a little break? So many unsettling issues in the marriage, finances, housing, and now a miscarriage! Not even the normal type I thought, it just had to be one of those where the child is still stuck in there. We were asked

to wait so we could hear about the options of getting rid of the fetus; my baby. I asked

"What options? Can the baby be saved? Are you sure "he" is dead?" The doctor responded

"I'm positive about this and I am sorry". I asked *"do you know when the baby died?"*, the doctor estimated between your 8th to 10th week based on the size and measurements but he said he could not be more specific. I died again, spirit, soul and body this time. I was given options of waiting until the fetus naturally got flushed out, or a Dilation and Curettage (D & C).

As we sat in the waiting room, various thoughts ran through my mind, *"God, why?"* I was too broken to speak. And when my ex decided to make a joke? I snapped at him,

"Are you okay? We just got news of losing a baby, I am waiting to hear about procedures and this is the best you have to say? How about a hug, how about you console me". I hoped for empathy after my speech but what I got was, *"Did you think I don't feel it, I don't want to talk about it, I know I am going to have children and so another will come."* I kept shut thereafter. The doctor gave us the options however he wanted a D & C to just get it out because it had been in there for about 5 weeks, not a healthy state for my womb. But then I thought, *"I kept myself until marriage and now I have to have an abortion? Nah! This child has to flush itself out".* So I declined a D & C. The doctor said he would have to put a date down and if I had

not bled out by the appointed date, I would have to have an emergency D & C.

As we went home, my ex tried several conversations but I just kept mute. As we got home, he said he had a client and had to jet, I told him I was hoping he would at least stay with me, he casually said we needed the money, and that he'd be back. As he left, I literally cried my eyes out. The grief I felt was beyond anything I had ever known or experienced. How was I even thinking we would be able to create a healthy baby in such a condition? In case you do not know, your state of mind, trauma, and sexual violence could cause you to have a miscarriage. Please do not stay in an abusive place. Do not even be pregnant in an abusive home, it never gets better. These are the things I did not know. Pregnancy was not going to change the way I was being treated.

The entire experience left me empty and I lost my will-power. It felt like I existed like "a walking dead". What was even more difficult was him not wanting to talk about it, or even allow me talk to people. I remember making a sneak phone call to some friend in Paris, and my friend detected something amiss in my voice. Sadly, that was my truth at the time. However, I could not tell him much about my living situation. It was my hope that these were challenges and that things would get better and it would become a mighty testimony. Besides, I was also taught to hide my spouse's incapability or flaws because it would be a shame to my family and I.

A miscarriage usually induces an intense period of emotional distress which could improve over a period of time with the right support. However, in my situation I had absolutely no support. No one to talk to, no shoulder to cry on, I was just always hushed down whenever I tried to raise the topic. Experiences like that could lead to depression and in fact post-traumatic stress disorders. I was going through a lot of traumatic events, but no attention or help was given and I just continued to function.

Chapter 4

PREGNANCY, STRIKE TWO!

A few days after the doctor's appointment, I began to bleed out; at that time, it was the most painful experience. It was physically and emotionally painful. A part of me actually hoped that a miracle would happen that this child would just wake up and continue living but one morning, I finally began to bleed. It was like pushing out a baby and it was painful because it was a dead fetus and not my baby that I could cuddle. All hopes of a miracle shattered. I bled continuously and profusely for three days or more.

He had always pressured me to have sex, and even in the course of waiting to bleed out he kept on but I stubbornly refused with the excuse of not wanting to start bleeding in the middle of intercourse, he on the other hand did not mind, while I had really painful contractions, and intermittently pushed out huge particles of dead fetus accompanied by much blood, it was interesting that it was on the 3rd day of heavy bleeding, massive blood clots and he was already asking if I was still bleeding that he *"wanted me"* It made me feel like all I was good for was sex. How could he be asking for sex at a time like that? All of this happened in April of 2012 and by Sept of 2012 I was already pregnant again.

The atmosphere was dangerous at home, and while he never hit me at the time, it was quite toxic with negative energy. We were constantly arguing and quarreling, one time I attempted to leave and he held my arms so tightly that his 'usually' sharp finger nails dug right into my flesh. He explained apologetically that he had to do everything necessary to stop me from walking out the door because, in his opinion, once anyone in a marriage walked out the door during an argument, the marriage was automatically over because they would never return. He always felt like he was a sage and had a smart answer to and for everything.

Another pregnancy, I was hopeful again that things could be different given the circumstances of the first pregnancy but boy was I wrong. The sex was more frequent and more turbulent than before. I remember asking, *"Shouldn't you be a bit gentler or less sex?"* These yet again fell on deaf ears. I remember thinking if he was probably trying to kill this one but had a rethink that perhaps I was really being melodramatic this time. Sex was a currency within our relationship, and he would say anything to me until I ultimately gave in to him. I felt too scared to speak until he had his way with me.

VIOLENCE, SEX AND THE FETUS

During this second pregnancy, it was suggested and I had to agree to keep it a secret because, he believed if I told anyone I would lose it. He had also constantly told me that there was something wrong with me and I was not supposed to be able to have babies because I might have been tampered with in the spiritual realm. He knew this because a supposed psychic lady in Australia had told him this. (I found out later that she was his online girlfriend but that is a story for another time). To be honest, the entire talk about my spiritual issues, made me determined and desperate to have this baby, I needed to show him that there was nothing wrong with me. I decided to stay calm, make myself happy no matter what it cost me. I literally said 'yes' against all odds. I had to preserve my state of mind. At a point due to my silence and non-resistance, it seemed like he just seemed to brew more trouble just to have a matter at hand; despite all I complied. These constant emotional and psychological imbalances I experienced found its way to the unborn child; this expressed itself in later years as the child grew.

The 12th week arrived, sonogram done and we got to see our baby. I was over the moon but still could not forget my first baby, whom I was not even allowed to mourn or talk about. Dating scan and other scans came and it was a boy. That December, I started a new contract role, and I was quite happy, anything to keep me away from the house. I was working, he was spending. The abuse increased but I managed, knowing fully well that in the morning I would be gone. At work, I got to meet people, research about pregnancy freely, make friends. This helped my state of mind. Home time as usual was a war zone. Pregnancy as usual came with its woes. From about four months I developed severe pelvic pains; I struggled to sit for long periods. I had headaches and back pains, yet all of this did not alter the fact that sex still had to be served on demand. I complained a lot, and he said, *"I have the healing power, my sperm is your healing, you just have to believe and stop arguing with me."* One thing the first pregnancy taught me was to protect my state of mind; it was easier to let him have his way than argue. By the sixth month, missionary style was absolutely ruled out and I had to insist that he stopped trying to lay on me. Every time we had sex, I said a quiet prayer; I could not afford or live through another miscarriage. As my belly grew bigger, it became increasingly difficult to seat for long, pelvic and back pains increased, coupled with contractions. Sex during pregnancy was awfully painful and if I ever complained he would snap out comments like, *"At this rate, are you sure you will be able to push out a baby, everything seems to be painful with you."* He usually made me sit in a particular position which he said was good for me but it was not, he would argue that the information on Google was wrong and wondered why I would trust the words of a random author over his. We carried on humping, arguing, stressing ourselves out while the baby kept growing and all tests seemed fine. I began to prepare myself for a vaginal birth; I always preferred being prepared, I dislike being taken unawares.

Sadly, by 33 weeks, the baby had gone into breech position and it was impossible for the doctors to perform an External Cephalic Version (ECV). We had to book an elective cesarean for 39 weeks. I was not fussed; I just could not wait to meet my boy. Looking back, it is interesting to note how much effort I put into staying sane as opposed to just walking out. To be honest, I did not know this was domestic violence. I was isolated from friends and family for the first year of marriage, we visited no one and no one visited us. I believed that every issue could be fixed, and I believed that this marriage would be fixed and we would look back and laugh at this very stage. After all it is not like he was horrible 24/7? I'm sure you have said this to yourself as well or heard people say this.

Back to my pregnancy journey, note that I did not attend antenatal classes as he believed that he had all the information we needed however it was just another way of isolating me. I desperately wanted to attend, at least I could pose some questions and maybe he would learn but he was smart, he could not have me interacting with anyone. It was now approaching my due date, I had stopped my contract seven days to the birth, just in time to shop for the baby and be ready. He took over the shopping hardheadedly, and spent ridiculous amounts of money on things that weren't necessary. Being a meticulous planner, I had mentally projected that a six months contract role that paid £36,000 in total, with a balance of £22,000 after expenses and debts, would cover me being at home for six months at least after birth or at least until I was ready to go back. I had a budget plan to cover the baby's essentials, cover bills, and daily living but he insultingly nullified all my plans with a *"Here we go, the project manager is here to plan everyone's life or Is it because it's your money?"*. As usual, I let go and let him manage the funds. I tried not to be stressed even though I could see that the bank account had no money in it and thinking after all that money made, we do not even have enough to keep us for a month and there's going to be a baby. Oh well, God will provide, I had a lot of faith.

There was a huge part of me that had given up on a lot of things, though I kept pushing, there was another part of me that just wanted to die and another part hoped that pregnancy would end my life and be free. I mean, people have complications every day, it wouldn't be strange. I was so tired of a lot of things. When I found out I was going to have a cesarean section, I was a little bit disappointed because I had read up that the process was less complicated than a vaginal birth. Heck! So I cannot even die in pregnancy.

Anyways, the night before the birth we had sex, I felt vile and I really hoped I was not going to come out of that theatre. I got shaved and washed and ready for my C-section. As I lay in the theatre, listening to the heart monitors beep faster, slower, and inconsistently as well as the voices of the surgeons, I prayed, and said, "God I'm ready." But I once heard a little squeaky voice and I knew my son was born. I heard the doctors say, *"She's losing a lot of blood"* and then I knew I needed to change my prayers. The thought of dying and leaving my son with him and some other woman revived my will to go on; then I became so scared of dying!

One significant thing about my son's birth that left me reeling in awe was not just that I felt all the tugging and pushing my belly around but when I heard the surgeon say, *"Don't pull, the umbilical cord is wrapped around his neck twice."* I couldn't and still can't imagine how it would have ended if my waters broke the night before; when we had sex, and my son pushing out legs first while being strangulated by the umbilical cord.

A SON IS BORN

A bouncing baby boy was born and he was perfect. I remember asking my ex, *"Are you proud of me?"* I really just needed to hear something positive as I was constantly made to feel like I was inadequate plus I know how people can be funny about cesarean section. He smiled, and said *"Yes, I am".* Two days later, I was back home again, optimistic that things would be different or favourable since there was a new born baby and we were now parents. I had just had a baby, my hormones where all over but contrary to my thoughts things went lower down the hill.

First of all, I was constantly put down when the baby cried, wouldn't sleep or feed. I wanted to feed exclusively except it was not possible, he did not want that. My boobs where bursting with milk yet he kept raging on about using formula milk. He said formula had to be the main meal and breast milk as a top up. All these subtly *mild* issues were very difficult to stomach. I had my hormones all over the place, a crying baby, a raging husband and I also started thinking of all the money spent without adequately stocking up formulas, nappies and baby grows. He bought quite a few branded outfits and shoes for the newborn who rapidly outgrew them.

It was not long after my son was born that the pressure to have sex returned with greater intensity. It was the third day of me being home, which was the fifth day after birth; I was sore, I felt every single pain from having my belly ripped open and stitched. My nipples were like raw meat from a suckling baby, and I was seriously sleep deprived. Only for him to say, *"I miss you with a rock hard erection"* I warded him off but then it became a nightly request. I had to remind him I had just had surgery and in pains, I peed in pain, farted with extreme caution, laughed, cough and sneezed with pains in my mid-section besides I could pretty much fall pregnant again, but he would make comments, like

"It's not as if you pushed out a baby, your vagina is fine and untouched."

At night, after barely managing to get the baby to fall asleep, as I lay down, he would often grab me, hold me, and kiss my lips and my neck despite my refusal. By the 10th day after birth, the verbal insults kicked with an insurmountable magnitude because I refused him sex. He accused me of frigidity, though I was hurt, I did not care having received a life's worth of insults since I got married; but what broke me was him yelling with those endless circular conversations which would wake the baby up. I needed sleep, peace and I did not want to have a sour or bitter mind while I was breast feeding. By the 12th day, he became a bit more aggressive about sex and I got fed up. I asked him to at least wait for my six weeks checkup or get a condom but he assured me he'd *"pull out"*.

Then one night it was unavoidable as I was exhausted from lack of sleep and the constant kerfuffle, he held me close on the bed and despite my recurrent objections he finally had his way with me. I was sick of arguing and fighting so I just laid there fully detached from the act. Once he was done I struggled to get up as I was in so much pain and had to be helped up. I got up, walked out of the room and sat in the toilet. I earnestly wished I could have a shower and just let the steaming hot water pour all over my body for over an hour so it could burn the smell of him off me and cleanse me. But that was not an option as my stitches would rip. I cried the whole time wondering what kind of marriage I was in. I wiped myself, checked myself as best as I could, just to make sure my wounds were not bleeding.

Yes I was fed up and had to give in, he did not care that my body was raw and broken after a traumatic birth. He did not care that I was too tired from having no sleep or a suckling baby along with other pregnancy complications, all he cared about was his needs. It was very difficult to achieve a sexual position that would not inflict excruciating pains. All his promises of being quick or the *"pull out"* never took place which created another fear in me of getting pregnant again.

Typing these makes me quite uneasy as I never imagined me ever narrating my ordeal. The stigma around rape needs to be changed. I was not out *'looking for it'* I was not wearing a short skirt and crop top, I was not drunk, I was not being a *'tease'*, which are the usual lines used to taunt rape victims. Here I was, in my own home, molested by my own husband. Did you know that most rapes are carried out by a perpetrator who knows their victim? This was certainly the case for me because the rapist was my husband. I did not even know you could be raped by your husband, and at the time I did not even realise that was what had happened. I lay down as he dozed off peacefully, snoring loudly like a freight train after the dastardly act, I wondered how he could derive satisfaction from my pain and tears. How can someone so composed, so soft spoken, a gentle man, also double up as this monster?

Sex again had become *a la carte* as he told me on a number of occasions that having sex would strengthen our relationship; I was not in the mood for arguments. So I placed the need of the child and mine foremost, if I expected to gain some sleep time, then the baby had to sleep too. I just did whatever it took to keep the peace at home; sex was the furthest topic from my mind. Sometimes, the baby would awake when we were at it, and begin to cry but he had to be ignored until we were done. It was a horrible experience, I was breastfeeding and he was sucking on me, this was not just disgusting but also very painful on my boobs that were still very tender. After sex, I would have to wash up, so that my son could suckle and fall back asleep.

THE DOWN SIDE OF IT

I would like to take a station break here to reemphasis categorically that sex without consent is rape. Being coerced into sex is also rape even if you are married. No one deserves to be ravaged without consent. I bet some of you are still trailing the line of thoughts like I did, *"I'll just do whatever I need to do to keep the marriage, and because of my kids"* but the truth is, it is not a pleasant atmosphere to raise a child. Your pain, your tears, cannot be hidden from your children. A typical example is, when I was pregnant, I watched Sky News a lot and the theme song would play before the news, at interludes and at the end. I watched Sky News almost every day from about 5 months pregnant until I gave birth. When my son was born, every time he cried and Sky news came on, he would stop and stare at the television. In fact he would stop whatever he was doing and be fixated on the television. This carried on, until about his fourteen month. Now think about being pregnant with your baby, all the arguments, all your tears, he/she hears and they are affected by your negative emotions and hormones emitted. This is exactly why you cannot remain in a toxic relationship. This is also why you cannot even think of trying to grow a child in an abusive relationship. You cannot hide it from the *silent watchers*. They see, hear and feel everything. Interestingly, over the past couple of years, research has proved that when you feel happy and calm, it allows your baby to develop in a happy, calm environment.

However, emotions like stress and anxiety can increase particular hormones in your body, which can affect your baby's developing body and brain. Excessive stress is harmful to your unborn child and women who go through severe stress during pregnancy can put their babies at serious risk. Domestic violence during pregnancy has been linked to consequent miscarriage, prematurity or low birth weight in infants. It can also lead future physical and psychological problems. Babies whose mothers experienced these kinds of toxic levels of stress while pregnant are statistically more likely to have respiratory and digestive problems, irritability, or sleep problems in the first three years of life. They are also more inclined to undergo developmental problems, with cerebral, intellective, social-emotional, and wellbeing issues that suggest neurodevelopmental substitutes that ripple into adolescence and adulthood.

Did you know that stress experienced by a woman during pregnancy may affect her unborn baby as early as 17 weeks after conception, with potentially harmful effects on brain and development? Cortisol, a steroid hormone, is pumped into the blood when we become anxious, in the short term, it is a welcome addition as it helps the body to deal with a stressful situation, but long-term stress can cause tiredness, depression and make an individual more prone to illness. If a woman is in a toxic relationship it will leave her constantly anxious and depressed this will automatically pump more cortisol that will be transferred to the fetus. And like most women in violent relationships who feel like they are *'walking on eggshells'* due to the fear of triggering any violent behaviour, physical injury or trauma, violence can cause stress hormones to rise in people exposed to the violence. So while I thought I was protecting my baby by remaining in that hellhole, I was inadvertently damaging my baby. Reminiscing about my first pregnancy, that dreadful miscarriage, I did not know or even imagine at the time that the violence that occurred while I was pregnant may have caused my stress hormones to go through my placenta and caused the miscarriage and premature death of the fetus. If you are in an abusive relationship, and it is impossible for you to leave, you can try these tips I tried during my second pregnancy:

- Leave the situation so that you can keep yourself and everyone else safe. This isn't running away, it is taking responsibility. An excuse like, *"I'm overwhelmed and I need to go out for a moment to settle"* could suffice.

- Before you go back, do your best to be calm. Take deep breaths or go for a walk.

- Tell yourself this, ***"Getting angry isn't going to solve this problem"*** or ***"I can work this out"***, anything optimistic would help you relax.

- Before you go back, feel calm in your body. The signs to watch for that express calmness include a deceleration of the heart rate, relaxation of the muscles and jaw relaxing (from feeling tense or clenched).

- While calming down, it might help to think about what set you off and how you could handle things differently next time.

If you find yourself in a situation like mine, where sometimes you just cannot or are disallowed to leave the house then this is a deadly situation, and you may end up with a miscarriage like me. You need to reach out to agencies and report your situation. You are not safe!

...AND THE DEPRESSION

Ever heard of Post-Partum Depression? Retrospectively, I probably had it but undiagnosed. We lived in isolation and I was hardly receiving any medical attention, being the strong person I was and still am, I just coped and kept going. Frankly speaking, I do not even know how I survived it all. This brings me to a question posed by my GP (General Practitioner) several years later, *"how are you still normal?"* Sincerely, I ask myself the same daily! I am guessing my brain just went into survival mode; so half the time I was on autopilot, just existing, just getting along, while hoping that the day would come when I could say it was all worth it and laugh at the past turbulent periods. Isn't that the hope of every victim of abuse, isn't that the hope of every

Christian? A teaching that suggests that such misfortunes foretell a future of testimonies. The more afflictions you persevere, the bigger the reward? This is why many good people, children lose themselves or even die in such trying life situations.

A new baby comes with a lot of emotional moments; joy, laughter, excitement and truly these moments existed from time to time and truth be told, I lived for those moments. Those moments kept me in the hamster's wheel: being hopeful. However, what was more prevalent was that I was nothing short of terrified. Terrified of what would happen to me, petrified of what could happen to my child, and terrified to let anyone know how fearful I really was. It is interesting how intimate partner violence works; it takes a few emotions to conquer fear, the most prominent of them is love.

Love makes us do crazy things. It drives us to endure when we do not think we can, it pushes us forward even when we do not even know which direction we are headed. I was overcome with love for my child. The other thing is what I have dubbed *"future faking"*; I was made to believe in an unreachable future. Future faking is one of the tactics of an abusive person, the hope, the promises, the apologies make you feel that there could be a path to connect to that sunny side permanently. Maybe, just maybe I had what it took to bring out the light in them. No relationship is perfect and so I never for once thought everything would be okay, I guess, I truly hoped that the coming of children would make things a bit more tolerable. As women or caring parents, we are tempted, ultimately brainwashed to stay in abusive or unhappy places for the sake of our children, we believe that the bad treatment and experiences would end with us, while the children will stay protected. Well that is a myth! The truth is that every kind of abuse you experience will be directly or indirectly experienced by your child.

NAMELESS

Our baby was born, looking gorgeous and a splitting image of his dad at the time but we had no name. Before he was born, I had asked several times about a name for our child but he was unperturbed. He said he was thinking about it, I found it awkward because I was used to couples discussing names and making a choice of them prior to birth. Obviously, there were some exceptions where people wanted to see their child first and be inspired to give a name. The countdown to the birth went from months, to weeks, to days and then the baby was born when we still had no name. It was quite embarrassing to me because when my family asked and a few friends that I kept in contact with asked, I had to tell them there was no name yet. I had to be the one coming up with excuses for things that were not done properly. Interestingly, because of the sort of person I was before marriage, most people listened and honoured my words. I think they saw me as someone that knew what she was doing, so it was assumed that all was well and I was on top of things.

Nearly two weeks after birth, the baby boy still had no name and so we resolved to call him *"lil bebe"*. He insisted it was a man's duty to name the child and he had to do it solely. He said he did not want to be rushed and that he had to research. In my mind, we knew when the baby was going to be born due to the planned Caesarean Section, we also knew we were having a boy, so what was the reason for the delay?

Finally, he gives a name, just at the mark of fourteen days. He gives a very good reason why he chose that name. I believed and was just happy we had a name. Interestingly, I found out from one of his friends months later that the story behind the name was false. We were outside church and one of the guys says, *"Madam Dot I love the name of your son, your husband has just told me about the man that inspired the name. I hope he grows up to be a great teacher like him."* I controlled my shock, smiled and just walked away. But wait, my son was named after a conspiracy teacher? Why? Also why was it shrouded in falsehood if it was that important? I also wondered if it was possible that he never researched on a name, but out of pressure and the fact that he had not named our son after two weeks, he just picked whatever came to mind. Anyways, it did not matter and still doesn't as the child had been named and we can move on to other things. There was immoderate nonchalance towards the child; I wondered why he was not as vigorous as he was in that regard as when it came to policing me.

Chapter 5

THE CONTROL FREAK

W ithin the first week of having a newborn, as I had projected inevitably, we ran out of nappies, formula, baby grows. Money had been spent on the wrong things since he believed that I would be called back to work in a month which at the time did not seem a selfish ask. Though I needed a break to really rest after my Caesarean section, I was stretching my faith that it would happen as he hoped. After all, if I did not go back to work, how would we survive?

Situations of financial crisis like ours were or are not that difficult to resolve, based on my status in the United Kingdom, I could have easily signed up for government benefits and have our rent, meals etc. catered for but he refused my suggestion, *"There would be another way"* was his constant mantra, he insisted it would not tell well on him as a husband, that it would seem life became worse off for me, to the extent I was seeking benefits. He reminded me that as a wife I needed to cover my husband's pride. At this stage of the relationship, I was already fed up of arguments,

I just needed peace. What I did not realise at the time was that claiming certain benefits required leaving the house and potentially interacting with others, and just maybe people may find out about the abuse or make me realise my situation, he could not have that happening. He would rather we suffered. Another thing about abusive people is that they sometimes like you to go through hardship with them, so that they can use it in the future to emotionally blackmail you with, *"After all we went through together"*

I had often suggested talking about our financial needs to friends, I mean any of my female friends at the time could have easily resolved our situation but he forbade me to talk to anyone. My mobile number had also changed twice in the first year of marriage, he had a good reason why we had to change it at that time but I just did not know that he needed to limit who had access to me.

When the time came for people to meet our baby, I was glad that members of the church would come with gifts, diapers, Baby Grows, cash, to mention a few, "At least that would keep us going plus I would have some company and see people" I thought. But it did not play out that way. One particular incident stood out for me. It was a visit from a church member, my ex's friend, Mr. Cassey. The visit lasted almost two hours, but I was not permitted to come out of the room because he opposed my interaction with men. As much as it was awkward, I still complied. I was not going to fight and lose peace over a strange man. Mr. Cassey brought along with him, packs of Aptamil formula milk, which had to be nothing short of a miracle because that was the brand we used. It was within the second hour of his visit that my ex came into the room to get me, subtly warning me as he said,

"You need to come and say hello to him but make it brief and give a good reason why you have not come out."

All of this was really distressing to me, my image was being tarnished, I had a bubbly, friendly personality but now I would be perceived as rude, and snobbish. Anyway, I made my cameo, said *"Hello"* and explained that I was really tired and the baby had been keeping me up. Mr. Cassey had kids, so I figured my excuse would make sense to him. As I took my leave back to the bedroom, I overheard Mr. Cassey telling him how blessed he was,

"My brother, you are very lucky, they no longer make humble, respectable women like this."

It felt good to hear that, as I had almost forgotten what a gem I was, constantly being put down and made to feel like I was good for nothing. Moments after Mr. Cassey left, I returned to the living room, and the first thing I noticed was the heavy breathing, stern face and veins on his forehead. I asked,

"Is everything okay?" his response was a stern question,

"Have you been talking to Cassey?"

The question was absolutely absurd as I had just had a baby; I had not left the house, and had no way of contacting Mr. Cassey. Next thing was to demand for my phone which I gave him and he spent at least, 40 minutes going through every message on it. I carried on unconcerned but still curious about what was going on. To my utter shock he comes back, screaming at me, that he knows I have been in contact with Mr. Cassey and expressed displeasure at my relationship with him. Meanwhile, in eighteen months of my acquaintance with Mr. Cassey, I do not think I had shared beyond a *"Good morning, good evening, bye, God bless you"* with him and all of this was under watchful eyes. I inquired repeatedly what the matter was and then he said,

"Mr. Cassey brought us Aptamil, how could he have known our child uses Aptamil if you did not tell him?" I was dazed as this was totally unexpected. So I retorted

"...but he brought us Little Angels© nappies and it isn't what we use. If I really told him what to buy, wouldn't I have told him about the nappy brand as well?"

"Oh here we go! The one that always has a smart remark, I know you've been talking to him and I need to know today what is going on between you two!" he said.

He was pacing back and forth and shouting at the top of his voice this woke the baby up who started screaming, unknowingly triggering my ex further.

"This boy will always start screaming whenever I need to get to the bottom of things."

I picked up our son and tried to pacify him.

"You need to answer me, how did Cassey know which brand of formula to get?"

I responded,

"Maybe because Aptamil is the leading brand in the U.K. maybe because his friend and colleague sister, Viviana visited last week and may have told him because she saw that that was what we use. After all they are work colleagues."

He carried on yelling and shouting and ended by saying he forbids me from using that Aptamil. As he declared

"I cannot have someone poisoning my child."

He stormed away to the bedroom and slammed the door. That again jolted our son and he started screaming, a very shrilly cry. I tried my best again to rock him to sleep and I also had to go check on my overgrown baby, he was still fuming, accusing me of being unserious with issues, that I would rather use the baby as an excuse, than resolve my marital issues. I had to pacify him by offering him sex with increased moaning for the sake of validation as was very important to him. After everything I told him, remember we hoped for a miracle, could it be a miracle that God told Mr. Cassey to get that brand...**WRONG MOVE!** That ticked him off again, but this time, I held him tight, caressing him and saying how I wanted him again because I was so horny. That was a big lie that it worked like magic and luckily, this time after round two he fell asleep. I snuck out of bed to check on the baby, fed him and put the formula away in the cupboard. There was no way I was throwing it away. I remembered imagining how that he would let our son starve, rather than use this milk. Like I said, directly or indirectly, children suffer.

Are you wondering about the milk? Well we ran out of formula milk and still could not afford to buy any so I was down to constant breast feeding. Now remember he had insisted on formula, and so my milk was not flowing as much as would be needed to satisfy a 3-week old baby. This also, meant less sleep for me, a very hungry baby, and I still had to fulfill my wifely duties. Finally, out of frustration and after rehearsing my speech several times in my head, I told him that we needed to use that milk Mr. Cassey brought. In my head I could not believe I was actually pleading for him to allow me feed our child. I had to use every single womanly, "whorely", "concubinely" tactic I had to get him to reluctantly agree with an, *"Okay!"*

Having every pleasant moment being turned into a sour one for no just cause was tiring. I never went for walks, never took the baby for walks, or mum and baby classes, all of these services are absolutely free of charge- He never agreed to them, he would say

"I do not want my wife and child influenced by public opinion; we are fine as we are".

It was not too long before I realised that having a baby was not going to be fun for me. All those dreams of going to the park with the baby and activities at the children centre were never going to happen.

PASTOR'S VISIT

I was informed that there had been an issue in the church and the Pastor, his wife and the leader of the men's fellowship were coming over to the house. I was not given much details but he told me he had been disrespected in the church. The team arrived, and I sat there listening to the story. First of all, what I was briefed on was different from what I was hearing and I had to control my shock and try to stay on the side of my man. Now at the time of this event, our baby was about four weeks old. The meeting started at about 9pm at night and carried on until 2am in the morning and the reason for the extension? Simple, they could not reason with him, he was not willing to be corrected. Remember that with an abusive person, they are always right. The meeting got pretty heated up when he got triggered and stood up in an intimidating way, swinging his arms and shouting down at the Pastor and his wife. I remember seeing the shocked look on their faces. Firstly, they were his pastors, secondly, they were at least fifteen years older than him, and three, they were expecting a dialogue and not insults spewed at them. I remember the Pastors' wife saying,

"Brother Dee you need to sit down while you are speaking, you need anger management."

Wow! That statement triggered him even further. They had never seen him like that, they had not said anything that would spark such a reaction and they kept staring at me. I sat there and said nothing. For sure I was embarrassed because of this behaviour and there was a baby in the house. The men's leader actually piped in,

"You need to keep your voice down, it's now midnight and you have a baby in the house" Oh more triggers! He raised his voice a notch higher, stating how they had no right to tell him how to speak in his house. At that point I heard the baby crying and took my leave. I did not actually want to be there.

But he came inside to get me to bring the baby out. He expressed his disappointment at my lack of show of solidarity, he had expected I join him in shouting back at the team. Basically, I do not believe in confrontation, there are many ways I can get my point across without raising my voice or exchanging words. I got the child out to the living room, and had to sit there with the baby for another hour of him lashing back at them. At a point the Pastor said he was leaving because he did not leave his house and give up his sleep to be insulted. The Pastor's wife urged him to stay and he stayed on. After all they came to resolve an issue which was still unresolved. I'm sure you are wondering what this unresolvable issue was... Ok here it is.

Worship was on going in church, a song my ex had suggested was not sang by the worship leader at the time he wanted it sung, and she went ahead to sing another song. He also suggested another song and then the Pastor changed the song. The men's leader noticed the angry expression on my ex's face. The men's leader spoke to the Pastor saying, *"I think we should meet with him, I've noticed he's not quite happy about something or some things."*

If my ex said a song needed to be sung, it was a massive trigger if it was not done. I had always made him understand that he was not the music leader in church, he was just a drummer, and that he should stick to his drums and that if he was asked about song selections, he should offer his opinion and back off. Telling the Pastor or his wife that they were not sensitive to the Holy Spirit or that they should listen to you is a recipe for disaster in any Nigerian or African church. With my years of experience in church, I knew for a fact that no instrumentalists' word could ever be considered above that of the Pastor. There's a chain of authority that cannot be broken. This was the genesis of the issue. His behaviour left our guests in utter shock, the pastor's wife constantly reminded him to keep it down because of the baby but he snapped at her,

"Do not talk about my child, he's fine." then he turned to me, *"Go and breastfeed him so he can shut up and come back"* I complied.

Looking back, I cannot even quantify the amount of trauma, the noise, the yelling, and the sleep disruption, could have caused my son. I cannot count how many times my son was woken out of sleep abruptly because of such situations at home.

After nearly three hours of fruitless and pointless arguments, the pastors left. You would think that was it. I settled the baby in his cot; I lay down and was on the verge of drifting when he taps me on my back, and told me we needed to talk. I knew the tone, he was breathing heavily, and I knew this was going to be another 1 hour of hurly-burly but what did I do wrong this time? He kicks off about how he expected me to join him to shout at the Pastors, that husband and wife are supposed to stick together. I tried to explain that I did not believe in hauling people over the coals, but dialoguing and talking calmly. I stated that, *"Once you raise your voice in rage at people, it will be very difficult for them to hear any points you make, all they will see is a violent person."*

Triggered! He sat up on the bed and began to lambast and castigate me, baby wakes up again.

WORD RAGE ...WORD SALAD.

There is something called a circular conversation, it is the kind of conversation that can go on forever when two people do not agree. In a lot of cases, people will say *"Let's just agree to disagree."* However, when you are dealing with an abusive person, a person with a personality disorder or a narcissist, you can never quite arrive at that point of agreement. They have to be right and even when you back down and agree with them, they are not going to be satisfied, they look for something else and go on and on and on. Raising children in such situations means that your child will not eat, or sleep until they are done. The reason people argue is because they have differences in opinion, and so when we do we are often trying to communicate feelings. However when there's tension in the air and we think the other person is not validating our position, we often feel too vulnerable to express our feelings. The bottom line is we will not be satisfied until we believe the underlying feeling beneath our statements is resolved, addressed or acknowledged.

When someone with a Personality Disorder starts with certain dynamics to a topic, you may just have the recipe for a never-ending circular discussion. That is because someone with a Personality Disorder is not always able to see the same reality that you see. To some people with Personality Disorders, the way they feel dictates to them what the facts are. My ex believed the people in church were undermining him (a word he used pretty often), he believed they were intentionally disrespecting him and he had a long list of reasons why he thought they acted in that manner. So his arguments with them or me were from a place of being disdained. At least that was what he believed. This can be described as 'Feelings Creating Facts'. The relationship and his reaction to things were wrapped around how he felt, if he felt loved, and then I loved. If he felt afraid, then I was dangerous. If his feelings matched up to my reality, then that would be a great moment! I would be wonderfully validated, incredibly appreciated, deeply and sincerely valued. At other times if he felt betrayed, I became the betrayer, and he needed to prove that point even if it took three hours to do so. In all that time, the baby stayed up.

SLEEP DEPRIVATION

As you know, newborn babies sleep more than they are awake. Getting enough sleep is essential for their development, it is the time when they can process their new experiences and skills that they are learning and wake feeling ready to learn some more. Sleep is the time for restoration and for children's bodies to recharge and retain the information they have learned throughout the day. Did you know that our body's energy is restored during deep Non- Rapid eye movement sleep (REM)? This is also when growth and repair takes place, it is also the time when brain development hormones are released. In the event that there is a scanty amount of sleep or splintering of deep sleep, this may reduce the amount of growth hormone released leading to developmental or growth problems in the unborn baby.

We have been repeatedly told that staying in an abusive environment is for the benefit of children, this is completely ignorant and destructive. I cannot count the amount of times my son was woken out of sleep day and night due to unnecessary squabbles. Infants are supposed to spend most of their first year of life asleep. Those hours are prime time for brain development, it is at that stage in life that neural connections are formed and sensory memories are encoded. However, when sleep is disrupted, as you will find a norm in most abusive homes, it does not only affect the abused but the children are affected as well. Now ask yourself, is it worth staying together with the abuser for the sake of the children and then end up with these kids growing up with insufficient sleep which would create several problems for them including decreased brain development, learning problems and more frequent negative emotions.

While it may seem a bit extreme and fictional, I do encourage people to take time out and do a ten to twenty minute online research on such topics to see for them themselves. Did you know that lack of infant sleep can also contribute to weight management problems; research has also suggested that babies are indeed affected by parental altercation and exposure to chronic conflict may affect brain development. My son was born with a large wobbly head, breathing issues, and soft belly muscles. Rather than listen to the Health Visitor (HV) who spotted these issues, my ex chose to argue with her, claiming he came from a family of big headed people.

Remember, you cannot hide your stress level from your baby, they can sense when you as a mother is distressed; stress can become contagious. Please do right by your baby, they are the future.

Chapter 6

BACK TO CHURCH

One morning and out of the blues, he says we are taking the baby to church on Sunday and I thought, *"Just like that?"* First, I ought to have been happy to go to church but, I was overwhelmed with unhappiness. I had a caesarian section that had not properly healed, coupled with some birth complications that required my being injected in the belly for the first 14 days, then there were issues around loss of blood, and my blood not clotting properly, coupled with a myriad of other things, I was not in the mood for a 'back-to-church' move. Also, there was this unwritten rule of going to church three months after birth. I could not understand the urgency, I tried to make excuses but astonishingly he insisted I got a new dress (Which he got!) my hair done and nails done too! It was not the normal visit to the hairdressers because he accompanied me there and stayed there throughout and while it looked romantic, in my opinion we really did not need to bring a two months old baby with us to the salon to sit in a buggy for three hours. It was important for him to follow me and monitor everything without considering that the baby at that age should have just been at home chilling. I just found it way too distressing.

Too many things crossed my mind, where did the money come from, why the last minute urgency? Scratch that! I'm leaving this house today and that is all that matters. It was when I got to church that Sunday I realised that we were in competition with the other couple that had their baby on the same day as me. He could not have them introduce their child in church before us. Also, we were not just church goers; we were the official instrumentalists for the church. However, in my few weeks of absence, some youngsters had joined the church and he thought they were taking our place. My coming back to church meant that we could kick them out. Now, I play the Keyboard, drums and bass guitar, I also sing all parts but one thing I do not do is hustle over who plays instruments in church. Not even in my teenage days. Besides, I had a new born baby, playing the instruments was just one extra chore, I was quite happy to lazy about at the back and just enjoy the service and gossip for once.

Going to church on that day was stressful for me, my body was still on the mend, there was a lot going on but I had to stick it out. As you know African church services have no time limit, it is as the spirit moves. We were now officially back to church and *churchly* duties. Typically, I had my hopes; I always looked forward to making the best out of situations. In my mind, I would go to church, relax, chat with the ladies, catch up with the other two women who had had babies, you know the usual, *"He doesn't sleep, he's growing, baby poo looks like this and that."* I imagined how I would have close friends help with caring and carrying the baby but again, I was a dreamer, a delusional dreamer in this matter, so to speak. An abusive person wants to control you and to stop everything that makes you happy.

After the first Sunday in Church, I guessed the attention I got was a bit too much for him. It was a phenomenal day. I had my way with words, so when I described how I almost died in that theatre while birthing my son, my testimony was BOOM! So, the Saturday before my next church service, I was lectured on how not let anyone touch the child, carry the child and so on. Not even the Pastor or his wife could carry the baby. This did not really make much sense to me. Please note that this was over ten years before Covid-19. I noticed the darkness in his eyes and I knew defying him would bring about unsolicited four-hours special edition brouhaha.

I was getting used to his mannerisms, when he was going to kick off and this one just was not worth it. I however decided that it would be nice if he told people what he wanted because I really did not want to be seen as this person that was being overbearing about her child. Suddenly he kicked off asserting that it was my job to protect my child, giving examples of how his brother's wife used to sanitize every single one of her child's toys that people touched and right in front of them; that was what he expected of me. Now I'm being forced back to church and also tasked with telling everyone to avoid my child. How would this even work when I would be up on stage playing an instrument?

That Sunday was mayhem, because I had to play the instrument, keep the baby in the car seat on the floor next to me playing the keyboard and intermittently telling anyone that asked to help me with the baby not to bother. I absolutely hated our return to church duties for these reasons, not only was it ridiculous, it made me look bad and unfriendly; the front area of the church had monitor speakers, with additional noise from the drums, that definitely wasn't a place for a newborn; and let us not forget that the baby had to stay in the car seat. It was in the heat of summer!

Several church members offered their help and then it was agreed after seeing how ridiculous that plan was that we left the baby in care of a lady BUT she must not take the baby out of the car seat no matter what. Being in church was frustrating, I was yelled at for not focusing on the baby, but how could I be right in front of the congregation, play the instruments and monitor the baby at the back. I tried hard to pacify and feed the baby ahead of the service with the hopes that the child would sleep through the service and so he would not need to be touched by anyone. It worked sometimes, but other times it did not. It was a complete disaster but what was freaking annoying was that people did not understand me and why I did not just accept the help offered.

Somehow the abuse you receive as a parent, your child will also get theirs in little or massive doses as the case may be. Another interesting thing was that he decided that he was the only one to give the baby a wash. Initially, it seemed fair since I had a Caesarian Section, but later I wondered to myself

"If I carried your weight during sex, giving my child a wash was not going to be that difficult". Weeks, months, and years passed and he still insisted I should not do it. There was always a reason,

"You are not healed... you cannot do it... this is my contribution to my child... a male bonding period... and you do not know how to clean a baby". It was highly frustrating to me because I could only be a new mother to this child once, and daily the baby was growing. What was most frustrating was that even when he was too tired to give the child a wash, he would refuse me doing it. It became like punishment and I could not understand the rationale behind stopping me from doing stuff I loved even though it directly impacted on the child.

I actually quite quickly lost appetite for being a mother, and I put all my energy into job hunting and getting back to work. What was the point of being a mother when, I would not be allowed to take my child for a walk? Virtually everything about the child had to be approved by him; my suggestions were not taken onboard. It was like nothing I did or said made the mark. *"I would definitely be making money if I went back to work"* I ruminated; I was definitely good at that for sure. Besides things were really tight financially and almost pointing towards potential homelessness for the second time, yet he still refused us seeking help.

3-6 MONTHS

As a new mum, I constantly focused on mum blogs and the NHS (National Health Service) website for weekly and monthly updates. I did not want to be missing out on anything the child needed, in terms of nutrition, activities and development.

It was now the third month after my son's birth and my parents had arrived to spend some time. I thought it would be a good idea, I could sleep without being woken up by the baby, maybe enjoy sex without waking up the baby, and I began again to dream. All the fun things I would do with my mum, and how she could maybe influence his thought process about staying locked up at home. Having a mother who was willing to offer a helping hand was nothing short of a blessing when you have recently had a baby with no help.

My parents visit was another rude awakening and I actually began to regret their visiting us. I thought and I really hoped that their presence would impact the way he treated me but it did not. As usual, I tried to cover it up because I did not want to get them involved. I had studied him for just over two years and I could see that he really had no regards or respect for anyone. When he was angry, he was angry. I could not have my parents insulted by him. In the course of two years of marriage, we left the first church because he shouted at the Pastor and had a few altercations with members of the choir, the second church we attended, same issues with choristers and then the Pastor, we got evicted from our second house because he shouted at the landlady (she was a senior citizen, a retiree and well over seventy years old), also had an outburst at the GP's office, at random cab drivers, and any other person who disagreed with him. So I knew for a fact that it was impossible for him not to show aggression towards my parents. Besides, even during their stay, he never hesitated to tell me off, rage at me in the bedroom. This was very embarrassing, the walls of the British houses are very thin, so I prayed my parents could not hear him every other night yelling at me. My mum had asked a few times in the morning but I covered it up.

All my mum's suggestions to take the baby out on a walk to receive sunlight, *"Baby needs to be weaned"* or *"Baby needs to sit up"* fell on deaf ears. He believed that he knew it all and everything done in that house had to come from him. I recall my mum saying to me,

"You are different; this is not you from just a few years ago when I visited. You seem not to be in the mood to do or try anything."

However, I covered it up with, with an excuse of how tiring and draining motherhood was. He insisted that my parents should never be left alone with the baby; this meant I had to hover over my mum, and at some point he said my mum should not be allowed to feed or bathe the baby. It was all too frustrating for me because, I recently had a baby, I had a man I was also babying and now I had my parents to monitor as well. My mother also became frustrated; I remember her asking

"Why did we buy a ticket to come and help you when I'm not allowed to do anything?"

Those words broke my heart, but as a true wife, a Christian wife I had to cleave to my man. One day I thought, things would be okay and we would forget all of these things.

He blatantly refused the baby being put on the floor and so my mum suggested spreading wrappers on the floor so that the baby could have belly time, if the floor being dirty was the issue. We tried it a few times but one night he kicked off about me allowing my mum run our home, that I should tell my mum not to put the baby on the floor any more or he would have to tell her himself. I also recollect an instance when his mum had called and he was asking her about issues we had with my son, the shape of his head to be specific. You see my son had an awkwardly shaped head because as opposed to carrying him, he insisted that if I was tired, the boy should be left in his baby bouncer seat. It was that seat that reshaped his head. I remember his mum saying, the head needed a massage and then she added, *"Your mother in-law is there, these are the things she can do for you or can she not do it?"* He immediately shut down the conversation.

In the African and Nigerian context, having an elderly person who was strong enough and willing to help a woman after birth was a gift. His mother could not understand why things that needed to be done were not being done; little did she know the conditions of our living. Sometimes, I wondered if it was his mum who had visited, if he would have restricted her as much as he did my parents.

I suggested that we invite his parents over, but he blatantly refused with the excuse that he was the sixteenth child, it would be awkward for him to be the one to invite his dad and mum, what would the other wives and children think? Well I did not understand the dynamics of polygamy and did not want an argument and so I suggested we invite his mum. He categorically stated that he could not live with her, and that his mum had said if she ever left Nigeria she was never going to return. In my head, I did not see why that was a problem! After all it is not like she was doing anything in Nigeria or that life was good for her. At least we would have permanent help and we could say we did something significant for her. But he got really angry and with a note of finality he firmly told me,

"She has a daughter abroad, that one can help her, and not me, I do not want her here."

A GROWING CHILD

We had gone through a lot of financial issues, from not having enough to pay rent, lack of food on the table or even baby formula. He still was adamant about me requesting government benefits of assistance. At the time, I thought it was just male ego like he had stated, it took a while for me to realise that it was solely because he did not want me leaving the house and meeting people.

The Pastor's wife somehow convinced him to allow me go for government housing which we did. Due to his immigration status, it had to be me applying and so I did. It was also at the appointment that they insisted I applied for government benefits. I recall the officer being shocked that I had never applied for any benefits given my circumstance. While waiting for the benefits to kick in, I got a job. I was over the moon. I was back in the game, making the big bucks and also hoping that the 5 months of hardship we experienced with a new baby would make him more financially smart. It was a good contract paying 255 GBP per day, as usual I had already envisaged a plan to manage our finances and pay up any arrears in household bills.

At this point I would like to say that a relationship should bring together two people who can complement each other. One person cannot have monopoly of knowledge. I was an accomplished Project manager, I managed high level budgets and financial plans, also, I had managed my life before him, without financial issues, or rent arrears, surely the finance of the family could have been better managed by me as opposed to him who had never done a formal job in his life, other than moving from place to place living off girlfriends and sugar mummies. Note this; the cravings to manipulate and control is fuel for an abuser, and he thrived on it so much that it did not matter if it affected our child. When it comes to domestic violence, the child is a disposable asset.

I came up with a plan to manage the baby and finance in my absence. I was back to work and the 'lil man' was only 6 months old. Normally, this plan was something that should have been easily achievable, after all when we were both at home, he insisted on being the one to bath the child, he had always yanked the baby off my grip on several occasions, asserting my ignorance in handling or nursing the baby, so presumably he was the expert because I had in fact began to believe I was not good at mothering. The baby needed to be weaned but the ex insisted that he had no time to feed a baby solids or anything outside putting milk in a bottle. You see I had taught my son to hold his bottle from a young age just to avoid being told by his father that he did not have time to sit and feed the boy. I also came up with baby cereal, easy to make in 5 minutes, and feed a baby with a spoon. He absolutely refused. It was interesting because all he did was sit at home for 10 hours while I was at work, so I wondered why he complained about time insufficiency and if he would rather have a malnourished child.

My ex had always made me believe he was not the traditional African man; he had no issues, cooking, shopping or baby-sitting. In fact these things, I was happy to do but he always insisted on doing them by himself. But suddenly he could not do them any longer because I was back to work. It was really difficult for me at work, thinking that all those hours my baby would live on formula milk and no solids.

He later suggested that the baby shouldn't be weaned and remain on formula milk until about 8 months. Leaving the baby till 8 months became unsettling because from about 7 months he seemed not to be satisfied with milk. I had to come up with a plan, feed the baby porridge at 6am before I left and then hoped he would at least do one meal 6 hours later so I could resume when I got back. All my suggestions were brushed aside and never considered.

I consulted a few online consultants, and they all said it was ridiculous to keep a baby for 10 hours on milk only to be fed cereal or food later. I showed him all the evidence but he still insisted that he was unable to do them. All of this took a toll on me and looking back now it still breaks my heart what my son in particular, was put through. Asides from not wanting to feed him, he never left the house. Thus, the baby stayed strapped in a baby chair all day while I was away and placed in front of the TV while YouTube played. He was never put on the floor to crawl; he just sat in a chair all day except when it was diaper change, or sleep time in his cot.

I remember asking if he actually liked his son… as many men, especially Nigerian men who had a first child as a son, and one who looked just like them, would be everywhere parading their child. At nearly 10 months, the baby was still not allowed to crawl, walk or go out to groups, parks etc, just at home watching TV. I put in extra effort to get him into physical activities whenever I returned, feed him age appropriate meals and read to him. Oh I read to him every day, even while I was pregnant. In return what I got from my ex was,

"You are neglecting me and spending too much time with him"

My bewilderment was unprecedented! Could he not see that I missed my baby whom he hardly had time for? The instant I vocalized my thoughts… Boom! Triggers for another 2 hours of rage, reproving me for ingratitude for all the effort he was putting in. I remember looking at my startled son, and how his eyes shone as he looked at his dad screaming. I thought to myself, *"this is not right, and I cannot have my son growing up to think it is okay to communicate like so"*

And so I decided to curb such confrontations, however when you are dealing with an abusive person, no matter how careful you tread on those eggshells, they will always find a reason to kick off.

Between 7 to 11 months of our son's life, I tried as much as possible to suggest things like going to the park, playground, swimming classes, and just interactive sessions for the baby; I also suggested that I could do them if he was not able or unwilling to participate. He would bluntly refuse alleging that he could never trust me enough to let the baby out of his sight; he did not believe I could handle a baby on my own. I suggested we fix child activities on the weekend and we go together. His next reason for refusing was that I was listening to too many women at work on how to raise a baby, and he was offended that I considered their words over his.

You see, my ex controlled my life, what I did, whom I spoke to, even up to what I ate. That same control was also seeped down to the child. I was isolated and so was the child. He would always sound genuinely cautionary when he told me to be careful with whom I spoke,

"I've seen this several times and before you know it, they will come for me."

He made me promise that if he ever got deported, I would come with him. He seemed to be quite apprehensive about people watching us, people being after him, this worried me because I felt there was more to it than I was being told, but he always assured me of his innocence. Then he would chip in bits of how his friends were jealous of him and how they could do anything to ruin his life, which was why he avoided them. Now I had met the guys from the barber shop, they seemed really pleasant and cheerful, absolutely nothing wrong with them, they were really respectful and I saw their good hustle. My man, who constantly put them down, did nothing for a living and just leeched on me. I got him into web designing, registered a company for him, bought all the equipment and got the first batch of clients. His friends on the other hand were handling their own businesses independent of a woman! Anyway, he stopped letting me accompany him to the barber shop because he was jealous of all the compliments I received. These men were literally thanking me for marrying him, they talked about how clean and decent he looked. But he hushed one guy, Bailey when he tried to describe the transformation between the past and now. These were his friends, if he said they were evil and a bunch of scumbags then maybe they were.

The need for him to control every single aspect of the relationship was incomprehensible. Had he been a financial mogul, a parent, or had he ever raised a child? No! So I always wondered why on earth he would not listen, even when there was proof that his choices were detrimental to the child. The answer is simple. It was the need to control me, and keep me in check and subdued, any other thing was secondary and not important. I soon accepted the fact that our child's only interaction with the world would be church services, and it was just being in attendance strapped down to a baby car seat for most of the service.

At about 11 months, the pastor had a talk with my ex, I'm thinking it was out of concern that other children born the same period with our child, some even much younger were already standing on two feet, walking or at least attempting to walk or crawling. He made a false excuse that he did not want the child on the floor and that the child walked at home. I remember the Pastor grabbing my son and putting him on his feet while holding his hands in an attempt to see him walk obviously my son's legs were not strong enough for that routine and he just wobbled. That was when the Pastor gave a long speech on allowing the baby crawl and walk, but most importantly the kind of foods to feed the child. Little did the pastor know that there had been ongoing arguments at home about the same topic of him refusing to feed the boy solids while I was at work.

That speech unlocked the door and he accepted giving the boy solids; he actually turned it around like it was his suggestion. I did not mind as long as this was happening. I also suggested getting a play pen. It was a big square and if the boy was kept in it, at least he could crawl around in it and try to stand up from time to time holding the barriers. He was not immediately keen but agreed when he saw the other boy who was born same day as ours, not only walking but dancing to Afro beats in *Azonto* style.

My ex being the competitive type, always acted like there was something to prove to this family who by the way were just going about their business, decided it was time to get our son on his feet. I did not care about the motive behind the decision, just happy about progress. We finally put away the baby bouncer and put him on the floor, the first couple of days my son just lay there, either on his back or on his belly then he began to wiggle and roll over.

A growing child comes with growing needs, how long were we going to cage this boy within the confines of our home, a walker tied to the dining table so he could not move? The things done to this child were a direct reflection of how I was treated. Since I was back to work, I had a breather for ten hours away from the house - hours of having people actually appreciate my efforts and tell me how awesome I was and that I was good at my job. I lived for those moments at work, I needed that validation to function and I craved it. It took my mind off the issues at home.

THE MYSTERIOUS ACCIDENT

My son began to pull himself up to stand, holding onto the playpen to take a few steps within the barriers, his legs got stronger and he began to attempt standing and walking unassisted. I spent a lot of after work hours, holding his hands and assisting him in walking around the house.

Due to the dynamics of our relationship and the fact that I was away at work, I had to text to confirm my location at the bus stop, when I got on the train, once I arrived at the office. I sometimes received hourly texts and calls which was extremely distracting. Sometimes he would ring just before I got into the office, find the littlest thing to berate me. There were times I missed a few meetings and even logged in late and I did not have any valid reason to give my line manager or colleagues. One time, I was at a meeting, giving a presentation, and my phone just kept buzzing even though I had informed him that I would be in a meeting, in fact he had access to my office calendar for the sake of peace. After my presentation, I had 20 missed calls and several text messages. I replied, letting him know the meeting would be done in a few minutes and then I could call. I also said if it was urgent he could message, but he insisted that it had to be a voice call. Next thing, he started messaging my work email which was embarrassing because I was logged into the presentation via my profile and messages began to pop up on the screen with titles like *"Pick your calls" "Don't ignore me"* and so on. These messages popped up on the screen in front of senior stakeholders so I quickly logged off. However, I was so uneasy, these kinds of messages left me with a feeling that something bad had happened or was going to happened. After the meeting I rang back, and he spent 40 minutes speaking to me in a manner of an indignant roar, spewing insults for my being unable to respond promptly. Stating that family came first and he did not care if I was in a meeting with the Queen of England, everything had to stop for me to answer to him. I still wondered what the urgency was and as usual, there was nothing really, just that he wanted to say *"Hello"*.

We were in touch and exchanged messages at least every single hour of my work day; break times were solely for him, if that kept the peace, then so be it! But there still remains a mysterious puzzle I was never able to solve. One particular day, we had conversed throughout the day, all the way to and from work, a 20 minutes ride from the train station to the house as was our custom. Barely 10 minutes from the house, when he suddenly mentioned that my son had an accident. I was a bit worried and asked how possible that was. He went on to say it happened at about midday, that the boy had tripped fallen over and hit his head on the metal base of his chair. I asked how bad it was and he said there was a dent on his forehead. Now this was shocking to me, as we had been in touch all day, and it was never mentioned for several hours, what really happened? Till this day I will never know why there was so much secrecy about the incident.

As a result of that fall he decided that the boy is not ready to walk and should remain in the baby walker. He also said the baby walker was hazardous and so he tied it to the leg of the dining table so the boy could not move about. I did not see any reason why this child could not be left to roam the house under supervision. It was not like he was doing things other than faffing about on Facebook. I came up with the idea that we should admit him into a nursery at least that way he could interact with other kids his age and my ex could have free hours since it was tasking for him to watch the baby but he refused... I even suggested a nanny yet all I got was a NO!

Sitting a growing child for most hours of the day was in no way good for his development. It was evident that convincing him to allow the child to interact or attend classes was a futile task. I was stuck with accepting the fact that the only other humans he would see would be on

Sunday, and even on Sundays, he was not allowed to be in Sunday school with the rest of the babies, he was strapped down to the car seat, slept in the car seat and fed in the car seat.

Just when I thought things could not get any worse, I could not imagine that our one supply of human interaction was going to be cut off. It was a Sunday after church service and there was a men's meeting afterwards. I sat with a few women, whiling away time before the end of the meeting. It was barely a few minutes into the meeting when my ex got aggravated and punched another member of the men's fellowship. It was unprovoked and unexpected; at least four men were trying to hold him down. *"Heck! This had to be the height of this embarrassing behaviour,"* I thought. I had tried on several occasions to tone down this character but never knew we would actually get to this stage. It was definitely bound to happen, after all in the past three months, there had been over three instances where he had disrupted the worship service and got pulled to the back of the church. Every time such happened, people always directed their gaze to me as if to ask *"Is he like this at home?"* or *"Can you do something to calm him down?"* I was unperturbed because I had reached a stage in the marriage where I was going to mind my business, and if, as we got home and he chose to take it out on me, then so be it. I was not going to team up with him in this unnecessary show of anger.

At this point, the Pastors and members were pretty much fed up with his frequent outbursts. The Pastor rang him few hours later and asked him not to return to the church because members apparently were scared of him and his behaviour. In his defense he said, the man had called him a stupid man, however out of the 12 men present, myself and 4 other women sat close by, no one heard this statement. It was maybe 3 years after this incident that he admitted that he hears voices. But we will come to that in a bit.

As opposed to apologizing for his violent behaviour, the decision was that we were not going back to that church or any other church. We had been married for 4 years and kicked out of 3 churches due to his attitude. He found the world guilty for trying to *'put out his light'*. Initially, I did not care about not going to that particular church, because it had become a massive chore for me. Managing myself, struggling to keep a toddler from interacting and exploring, also avoiding building friendships with people because that would trigger him and particularly the fact that certain people acted funny towards me after I came back from maternity made me uncomfortable. I did not know what had transpired in my absence.

An abuser wants to control and manipulate you and also manipulate the way people see you, so while you are being loyal and trying to be the virtuous woman to save your marriage; the abuser is thriving on that. He is also tarnishing your image unbeknownst to you; they will happily throw you under the bus instead of others, if it makes them look the better person. The same behaviours towards you will affect your children. Do not forget the children are also watching and parents are the first example they emulate.

We stopped church, and that was the end of interactions. At the time I still had my job, so I enjoyed my 10 hours away as much as I could, but I could not help but pity my son who had to sit at home, every single day of his life. I believed him when he had told me that the boy was still young and with time he would go for child activities, but little did I know that was just a promise of a vague future. We were not like the average family that had friends and family visit or even events to attend like birthdays or weddings; we just stayed at home all day.

Do not stay in an abusive relationship for your children; leave an abusive relationship because of your children. They deserve better.

Chapter 7

CLOSET NARCISSIST

I never really understood what a or who a narcissist was until I left the marriage, then suddenly everywhere I turned, this word was thrown at me, and I could not figure out why I never came across it. The fact is a narcissist will tell you things that are true in an implicit way, they may even tell you they are a narcissist but you would not believe it because you are not quite at that place to understand it.

In my case, it was one random afternoon, he was on his computer and I sat holding our son when he asked, *"Do you know what a narcissist is?"*

"Nope" I responded airily with no firsthand knowledge of what that was. He said, *"Come on, you are really smart, I'm sure you've heard of it or just take a guess..."* then I replied,

"I'm completely clueless but based on what I've watched and heard it mentioned on Criminal minds (The TV series), I think they are serial killers. They believe they are never wrong, and justify why they have to kill people. They also like to be

acknowledged, which is why sometimes the investigators apprehend them by acknowledging their sadistic skills, or giving credit for their crimes to someone else to make them jealous, and then they will turn up to admit to it."

He smiled slowly,

"You were pretty close. They are not always killers but the rest of your definition is close." I got inquisitive,

"Why are you asking about narcissists?" to this he responded in a spine chilling tone

"I just did an online questionnaire and it says I am a narcissist."

Unsure of what was really transpiring, I laughed saying,

"Really, well that's not good I suppose?"

The direction of the conversation changed drastically when he snapped, *"This is the problem with the world, a narcissist is a person who's awake, and doesn't conform to the norm. Why would anything be wrong with someone who is always right? Why should I be branded because I am right and intelligent etc? This is just absolute trash."*

Right there and then he told me he was a narcissist but I was unmindful of the weight of his words. I was thinking serial killer but maybe just maybe if only I had researched the topic a little further. Just like domestic violence; most people think towards physical violence and monsters but not the subtly abusive ones, the emotional, the financial, and the psychological ones.

He had this thing going which I never understood, this need to be worshipped by his family, by friends, church members, and acquaintances; this need to be seen as someone to be revered. I was taught that you had to earn respect; it was not to be forced out of people. But here I was with a person that every time his ego was bruised a little by anyone he started a storm. He would spend so much money just to win adoration from people and when it did not happen, he would go into rage. How he neglected us, the baby and I...his family, just for an ego trip was cryptic to me. We were unkempt and lacked a lot of things. Yet we were spending frivolously on random, unimportant things like throwing a party for the Pastor and his wife, individually, bearing costs of printing materials for the church, and equipment purchase, yet we lacked rent and food for the child. For instance, for my son's first birthday, he insisted we threw a massive party for him. I saw no point in this because his estimate was going to be over three grand, which was about my monthly pay at the time. We could have catered for the same amount of people at a quarter of that cost, but Hell NO! He needed to prove to the church, he was a big boy financially, and of course the other couple that had their baby, were also throwing a party, so we needed to compete. He also wanted to show his family how well he was doing. But what he failed to tell these people was that all the money came from me, and his lifestyle was putting us in poverty.

He would buy branded clothes for my son just for picture purposes, even though the boy hardly left the house. Now while he had branded clothes, he lacked the basics, like panties, vests, PJ's, age appropriate toys and books etc. It was all about making a public image. Just like in public, we were the perfect couple, all loved up.

Some narcissists, **narcs** as they are sometimes referred to, may have an underlying sense of insecurity or fragility, they can also have a grandiose belief without doubt, that they are special, unique, and superior.

- Are you with a person that longs for admiration, lacks empathy, has an exaggerated sense of importance?

- A person who has persistent fantasies of increased success, power, happiness, love, intelligence, or physical appearance with a belief that they are so special that they should only associate with other special people?

- Does your partner have a belief that they should receive special attention, treatment, and gifts?

- Do they have a tendency to take advantage of other people or situations to fulfill their goals?

- Are they lacking care, compassion, and empathy for others, while being envious of others and thinking that others are envious of them?

- Do they appear arrogant, conceited, or self-absorbed?

If you have affirmed to a couple of these, then you are with one of them.

KNOW THEM

Grandiose narcissists will also display very high confidence and self-esteem, superiority and entitlement, impulsivity, anger, hostility, and verbal or physical aggression when confronted. This was why we not only had issues at home but in public when the church, the doctors, the taxi driver, the dentist, the shop attendant etc did not give him that sensation.

Casting my mind back I can confidently say we were dealing with everything on the afore-listed. If you are with someone displaying a good percentage of these then you really need to take a step back and rethink your strategy. I do not know any narcs that have changed, and stayed changed. Do not grow old waiting for your partner to grow up, or change. Do not invest your life and that of your kids in a never ending adventure of trying to change an unchangeable person.

Emotional abuse could be very subtle, but narcissistic abuse leaves you anxious, depressed and confused about reality, it leaves you confused about the situation. Narcissistic abuse and emotional abuse will affect your child just as much as it affects you. Here are some signs of emotional abuse that will affect your child just like it did mine.

Extreme jealousy: The extreme jealousy your partner feels will extend to your child and/ or children. They are not willing to share you with anyone, they want all of you. The abuse usually gets intense with the arrival of a child. Sometimes, you will be forced to neglect your child for them, you may be asked to choose between them or the child. I could never understand a man being horny and staying fully erect when a baby is screaming high pitched, and insist on his needs being met over the baby. A baby could be pacified in a few minutes or at the most, hours, while a penis can be re-erected in two minutes with only a few strokes! They will kick off arguments over nothing if they feel that the baby was distracting you from them. Countless times I was being told that I spent too much time with the children, or that I should understand that without him they would be non-existent.

Possessiveness: Abusers are very possessive and again this can extend to the child. I was not allowed to attend mum and baby groups or interact with people which meant that the baby as well would not interact. I did not go for medical checkups except in extreme circumstances. I had to give him at least 48 hours' notice before ringing my doctor because he told me never to book GP appointments on the go. These rules extended to our child because in his mind I was making up excuses to leave the house. There was a certain time my son's teeth were looking discoloured, I wanted to go check it out with the doctors, but he maintained I stay home and use salt. You see, if he could not come with us, we were not leaving the house. I always mentioned my son's breathing; I am asthmatic, so I could tell even without a medical background. He vehemently refused checking the boy out, rather went through other methods, like lemon, Calpol, Calcough and all the *Cal* brand medication. Finally, my son ended up in a code blue ambulance alert and straight to emergency. It was in that hospital admission that my son was diagnosed with asthma.

A bad temper: Shouting at their partners, threats of violence towards the victim and justifying it by blaming. Remember that for every temper tantrum and outburst of your abuser, the child will witness it and that affects their cognitive development. They will dismiss your feelings, treating it with levity; this attitude will turn up with the child. Even when your child is crying or needs attention, you will be asked to ignore the child and focus on them. The needs and feelings of the child will be ignored just as much as yours are. When my son got a bit older, he began to display a lot of sensory processing needs. Tiptoeing, flapping his hands, need to rub and touch stuff, sometimes lick things. His dad would absolutely freak out in rage if the boy touched something that had a bit of dust on it or when he licked stuff. The boy would stare vacantly, not understanding what went wrong.

The NARCISSIST is worse when a child is born. That rage lies dormant like a sleeping dragon and then flares up unprovoked. Your sleep or your building milk supply doesn't matter. The baby is an extension of their quest for supply. At all developmental phases, the baby, a growing individual; must reflect his image or will receive his rage. It was always an issue if anyone likened anything about the child to me, especially in resemblance. The child must be perfect or it will receive his rage. I was convinced that pregnancy was used to control me, I thought more about *"Stay for your children most time"* and the supposed impact of children growing up without their dad or a broken home. I love my children but I know they were only premeditated and produced as a means to manipulate and control me, a proper narcissistic supply! He was always quick to say, *"I will never let you take my child out of my sight, not even if it is just across the road or to the playground, never!"* Even though at the time we pretty much lived in an area with an amazing green space, 3 massive play areas with equipment, a Children's Centre equipped with a sensory room within 5 minutes' walk and four baby groups in operation, I/ we never took the baby boy to any. In addition to that he absolutely refused to let the baby crawl on the floor. His reason was the carpet was dirty. I found this statement utterly shocking.

Now back up, while I was pregnant and working, he insisted on doing up the house. I was not in agreement because it was a rented flat. He wanted to have the flat repainted, doors refitted, re-carpeted. Now these were good ideas but it was the duty of a landlord, and I could not fathom why. He firmly asserted that he could not wait for the landlord. I was working and there was money, and I could not stress about it, I was nearly seven months pregnant at the time.

He not only proceeded to re-carpet the entire house; he did so by a high ranking household company. I remembered coming back, and everything had been changed, then he proceeded to change the sofa in the house, after spending

500 pounds on it, decided that it had an odor, threw it away and bought leather set again for 3 times as much, dining tables, beds, curtains, and wall hanging etc. Now the flat was not an unfurnished flat, so these things already existed. It was quite heartbreaking at the time but also impossible to argue when he was a certified *argumentator* and would not hesitate to throw in the guilt card, *"Is it because it is your money?"* In addition to that, he insisted on new equipment for his graphics, which made little sense but I thought since the graphics does not bring in much, the available laptop could work in its stead; but again I chose my peace. He had access to the accounts and as usual went the whole nine yards.

A new computer, new table, chair and then proceeded to build a music studio in the guise of keeping me busy after giving birth. Tempting but again, I was content with the keyboard I already had; I did not see the point of replacing it since it worked. I knew what my income was, and it was the only income between us both. Spending at this rate would mean we would struggle after I gave birth. Yet he proceeded and bought a keyboard, mic stand, mixers, AI feedback speakers to mention a few and then took pictures of the studio and sent to his friends.

Dear ladies and gentlemen (as the case may be), never let anyone that contributes so little, take control of so much. He was a financial wreck, on a mission for self-image, grandiose and not **us**, in a personal competition to prove to his family, (especially his younger brother) that his life was way up there.

Back to our son's prohibition from crawling at the age where he had to, with the flimsy excuse of a dirty carpet (that we just changed two months ago for the purpose of having a baby that would need to go on the floor? He also got a brand new TV; the latest LG smart TV at the time, glass centre table amongst others. I came home and was shocked, he said we would be having guests after our son was born and he wanted the house looking fly. Few months later he said in passing that he remembered few years ago walking past an electronics shop and saying one day he would own a Plasma TV, he cannot believe he had the latest brand.

With a narcissist, you may think the relationship is about you both, but seriously it is a ploy to achieve their personal desires. Children are bargaining pawns to keep you and make you believe you have a family. Any reasonable person would have been thinking about the baby's survival and not spending thousands on irrelevances, and then having a child and instantly struggle with little money to buy pampers and formula, unpaid rent also accruing.

Also, because I was always *notoriously* employed with a fat pay check, I did not mind as much, I was confident that I could easily get a job. I did not realise that these sorts of relationships came with a package of bad luck and that myself and unemployment would become siblings and getting a job would not be as quick and as easy as it was in my past life.

Ridiculous amounts of money were still being spent extravagantly, we had paid nearly ten grand in a music video shoot. What did not make sense was maxing out credit cards, cleaning out bank accounts for a music video, and then struggle to pay rent of £750 at the end of the month? How absurd! So I decided to change jobs; perhaps if I earned a bit more we could have a bit to put away in savings or investments. I secured a new contract which meant bagging £3500 every 10 days. As soon as the first wages for my new role came in, I was thinking about clearing out some of the debts accrued from the previous music video from only just 4 months ago, he came up with one venture or the other.

First, he needed to invest in a business for his mum that cost £2000, and because he was doing that, he needed to also give £1000 to his dad so it would not seem awkward. I was not going to argue. Money kept being dished out as earned and of course the basic needs of the family remained ignored. We also needed to buy his younger brother a car, reason being that it was not good for him to use public transport with two kids. Later on he needed to send his brother abroad, and so we kept moving large sums of money to an unknown source. He was planning to send his brother abroad and made his brother promise not to tell his own wife! Some of these things did not make much sense to me. I was up for helping but let's take a closer look.

Were we helping his brother because we wanted to help or was it just to show that we were better? His brother at the time had two jobs, his wife worked, they lived in a 3 bedroom rented house, and to the best of my knowledge did not owe any rent like us. His brother funded his own marriage, but here we were trying to help someone that if he truly knew our situation would most likely reject our help and ask us to help ourselves. I paid for our wedding, we did not have a car, we had a child and one on the way yet it was more important to get a car and later on a bus for public transport for his brother; someone who could afford it. We struggled with rent most times; these guys were fine with their rent. To be honest, his brother was doing a whole lot better than us, and he knew it which is why he always looked for ways to prove that he was better.

About a month later, it was decided that we needed a new music video. This video cost £20,000(GBP)!; which was everything I had worked for, and I even took a few soft loans here and there. Do not get me wrong, if one had gotten some endorsements that paid for these, then yes. But doing this and not caring about home supplies was unquestionably senseless. These actions were taken just to prove to his family and friends that he was way above them. Now the church was our enemy and so we had added them to the list of people to show that we were better off than they. Besides, we needed to spend that much because our video had to match up with the likes of Afrobeat legends like DBanj, PSquare and Tuface. These people were millionaires; they had several endorsement deals so how could he even want to compete with them? It was that self-inflation, the grandiose that he was special and a star but all at the expense of the family.

Please note that if you are with one of such people, you will experience narcissistic abuse and the effects on children witnessing these episodes is a risk of developing mental health problems such as PTSD, anxiety disorders, or depression. They might become frightened in situations that remind them of their horrifying encounters. They might also feel enraged at your partner or the world, feel detached from other people, or have low identity or morale issues.

Chapter 8

PREGNANT...THE THIRD TIME!

S everal months of not going to church meant, several months of zero interaction for my son. To be honest, the thought of it weighed me down daily until I just gave up thinking about it and hoped that the infamous *"one day"* will come when he can be registered in a pre-school or nursery.

By April 2015, I had just completed my current contract role with no extension; I was aware of the budget, I knew there was no possibility of an extension. We had more issues around finance. He had blatantly refused to work, even though it had now been about seven months since he had received his immigrant's right to work, so I really could not reason out his refusal to work. This was the same person that had told me so many stories of how much of a hustler he was. Well, I had been carrying the family for 4 years on my own, and money was being spent haphazardly. Whenever the topic of work came up he had a reason or two. For instance, he needed to take his time to decide on what sort of jobs he wanted to go for, another time, he did not believe in both parents working and leaving the child with a child-minder. I reminded him of my concluding contract which meant I could be the parent at home if that was the case. At a subsequent time, he shared his dream of studying for a Master's degree and as a wife he would have expected that I paid for it. He chimed that every member of my family had a Masters and if I was a good wife, I would push my husband, him, forward. That degree for him at that time would have cost at least thirteen grand (£13,000), which I would have happily paid for even though I saw no sense in it, but the fact was my contract was coming to an end. I came up with several savings schemes to put savings away, invest in trusts for our son but all was to no avail. He had his plan and I had to comply.

Between December 2014 and April 2015 I had made a total of £50,000 (GBP) however, at the end of my contract in April we only had a total of three grand left. There was always one white elephant project to pay for, or one relative at home with an issue, one church event that he wanted to sponsor, I'm still pretty pissed at spending over 20 grand on a music video, lodging in 5 Star hotels for gigs and also lodging the dancers, who were paid for their performance in the same 5-star Marriott hotel.

Now do not get me wrong, I'm up for charitable works, investments, but throwing away money is on a whole new level. Furthermore when an event is organised in competition with another brand, it becomes baseless, because these extravagant financial escapades left us in financial deficit several times. It was quite severe at some point that we could not afford food to eat or feed the baby. But I was told that my lack of belief in the investment was the cause of its failure.

A HOLIDAY FROM HELL

Holidays are amazing but sometimes they could become a holiday from hell. My family was notorious for ever being late for everything but little did I know that we could be so late and miss our flight. Yes indeed. At the time when we were to make that journey to Heathrow Airport, in fact the cab was already outside, that was when he decided to turn on the keyboard and have a family worship. I kept suggesting that we could just say a short prayer and leave. He got agitated and I kept shut. We sang worship songs over and over with lots of prayers committing the trip into God's hands while ignoring several incoming calls from the cabby alerting us that he was outside waiting.

Finally, we rushed down to meet up with the cabman before he left in disdain. I remember him asking what time our flight was and then shaking his head indicating that we would need a miracle to get there on time, that was the same thought I angrily nursed yet trying not to show it, we arrived the airport and not only had we missed check-in, boarding but the entire plane had departed. I was deeply infuriated. I never wanted to go on this trip because I was out of contract, we had spent nearly 20 grand on a music video so logically I should remain in the U.K. trying to secure another role, since he was unwilling to work; but now, here we were spending what was left on a trip.

I did not want to experience any more suffering; neither did I want this child to go through anymore unnecessary hardship. We were told we had to get another ticket for the next day at half the price, he whipped up a storm as usual and I remember my son staring at him while he yelled at the attendant. She calmly said,

"Mr! the plane has departed, I cannot bring it back. You can go home and rebook another flight for tomorrow or look for alternative locations in the USA and make your way from there."

His option was to lodge in the airport and I was like, do you realise how expensive that is? Anyways, we found another flight but this time to New York later at night and not Maryland our intended destination. Our son was getting really agitated and I had asked repeatedly for him to be let out of the buggy. At the time, the little lad could walk; he was nearly two years old, so there was really no need keeping him strapped down all the time.

It was interesting how an eight hours journey to Maryland became a twenty six hours ordeal. We got to New York late, there was the option to join a coach to DC, however he chose to get a cab. It was his first time traveling to the USA, it was his second time on an airplane yet he would not listen that it was way too long a distance to cab it from New York to Maryland. In the confusion we missed the next two available coaches. My worry was the child, we were running out of formula milk, and baby cereal and snacks were all gone because I only planned for an eight hours trip.

There was another coach we could catch at a different location so we headed there, in the midst of trying to get there; he decided to take pictures of the sites. An abuser is selfish, they think of themselves. It was going to be an entire 2 weeks holiday and these sites would always be there, I would have thought the more logical thing to do would be to get to our destination so this child could rest properly. My son had been awake for several hours, half the time strapped down which was uncomfortable. By the time we got to the location, we had missed the third coach. As an adult I was myself at my wits end, I was fatigued, irritable and sleep deprived. I could not even imagine the impact on the child.

Finally I thought I would get some well-deserved rest, we were in a family house, with familiar people that had, five adults and three children. Not only would my son get a bit of interaction, I too could get a bit of break from mummy duties: false hopes yet again. I was instructed that the baby had to be within my sight at all times. Everywhere we went we had to take him.

A scenario that did not make a lot of sense to me, coupled with the stress on our two year old, was making a trip to New York. This trip was not for sightseeing but for business. We were scheduled to see a music promoter and took the two year old with us. Firstly, there were more than enough hands to leave him with at home, but no, we took him on a journey that would last for over 4 hours. On getting there, it was hot, summer hot, I mean HOT! The little lad had to sit in the buggy in that heat for nearly two hours of the business meeting. Even the promoter asked a few times, if we were going to let the boy out, and of course we made up excuses. After the meeting, I had to quickly find a spot for nappy change, insist on letting the child out for a bit as he had been seated for hours. We had a limited amount of time to be at the coach stop to get back to Maryland, but again you know we were notorious for never being on time.

After faffing about New York with an agitated baby, it was time to make our way back. We had limited amount of time. As we made our way back, he decided to make multiple stops to take pictures. I kept reminding him that we did not have that much time to keep stopping. We could always come back but he insisted. Finally, it was time to literally run to the coach stop. There I was pushing that buggy while running like my life depended on it and then boom, he stops and says he knows I am hungry and we should stop at Burger King. I quickly said, *"No I'm not hungry I would rather catch the coach and get home to a nice meal than stop at Burger King and miss the coach."* I mentioned that the child had been on the road for too long and we needed to get him home as soon as possible. He then suggested that I should make my way to the coach stop, he was sure the coach would be late or that I could persuade them to wait for him while he went to get some food.

By the time I got to the coach stop, they were already boarding, of course the driver said he could not wait. I was almost tempted to leave him and go on my own with my son. But then I thought about what would happen when he got home. I was not ready for that. I pleaded with the coach driver and he waited an entire 35 minutes yet no sign of my ex. It was at that point they had to leave. I still waited another 20 minutes before he turned up asking if they had left. I was livid. Then he said it was not a big deal that there would be another. We sat in the sun as there was no shelter or shades with our child on the floor and waited another hour and half for the next coach. While I was frantic about getting home, he was unbothered and calm.

The thing with these coaches was that, we were not priority because we had missed our ride. This was down to availability and if some passengers did not turn up. The coach arrived, and of course we had to buy another ticket. He got into an argument with the coach driver when we were told that there were no available seats for us as a family and that he had to be on the lower deck while I had to be on the upper deck. He kept arguing that he could not separate married folks. The driver got irritated and informed us that if we missed that one there wasn't any other for the day. I intervened and he agreed that we got on it. Now while you might think, *"Awww... he wants the family to be together"* it was more about being able to monitor what he thought I may be doing, who was seated next to me and who may be talking to me and if I was going to be on my phone or not. He considered all this over us getting our child home and well rested. The necessity to control the victim will cloud their judgements to make the right choices. Scratch that! They are not really interested in the child, you the victim, are the most important pearl. Anything and anyone else is disposable. Know this and know peace! We left for New York at 6 a.m in the morning; we got back at 9p.m at night with a 23 months old baby.

BACK HOME

We went back to the United Kingdom, all stressed out, even more stressed out than before. As usual, my head was spinning due to the money spent and how we would survive. He on the other hand, was on Facebook with friends, clients and family talking about how he had just taken his family to the USA. That was laughable, a trip paid for with my money? And why was it so important to tell the world? I didn't think going to USA was a big deal, I had been there several times, besides, why make it a big deal when literally there was no money to pay the next month's rent?

He was very confident that I would land myself a new contract and then the spending spree would continue and he made it quite clear that he was not going to work. He wanted to stay home and deal with his online clients and take care of our son. I started on the job market, application after application. In the course of doing that, I realised I was pregnant.

Now after our first born child, he made it quite clear that he was not ready for another. I stayed on the pill until after over a year of pleading, he agreed that I could get off the pill and it still took another year plus or so for me to get pregnant and I was over the moon.

I carried my pregnant belly going for job interviews, one after the other until about the eight month. I could not imagine how he could sit at home so comfortably waiting for me to get a job, while I made all those long journeys with my big belly. For one particular interview I traveled a total of four hours to and fro while he sat at home. I was pregnant yet there was no concession. He still insisted he was taking his time to decide on the best option for himself. Things were bad; we were already in several months of arrears. I dared not talk about pregnancy craving as that would tick him off with the insinuation that I wanted to ridicule him that he could not provide. Well after my eight month in pregnancy, it was unrealistic going for interviews, who on earth was going to employ me at that stage only for me to go on maternity a few weeks later. I could have claimed jobseekers benefits due to unemployment but he refused! He did not want me interacting because that was the one benefit that would require me going into the benefits office every Friday to sign up. He would rather we starved.

In my second pregnancy, the baby went into a breech position at 35 weeks, I could not at the time prove that it was due to the positions he made me sit and the sex but this time, I got to pose some questions to the midwife since he was not in attendance. And I remember how my heart sank when she said, *"I do not know where you are getting this information, but this is harmful to your child, and can cause your baby to go into a breech position."* I always knew he did this to me, and now I had heard it firsthand from a professional. I went home but did not have the guts to tell him, I did not want another argument.

Domestic violence is not just a crime to you, but a crime to your children.

THE ACCIDENTS

Between the ages of 18 months to three years old, I noticed a pattern that every time my ex went into his conversations of rage, my son would stand in the corner and wet himself. Now it gets worse because he proceeded from not just having a wee accident to pooping on himself.

The terrible thing about it is that my ex would refuse me changing diapers insisting he was not done talking, that I had programmed my son to do this whenever he was talking so that I would distract him and stop him from having his say or getting to make his point. How ridiculous was that? Programming a two year old? I once said,

"Have you considered that he may be scared?"

But that triggered him further. My son had to stay in his wee and poop, and wouldn't be changed until whenever his dad was done talking.

You see, the rage was not just towards me, it was just the way he was. He was raging at the top of his voice to his mother, his sisters, his brother, his clients. Initially I was opposed to the way he spoke to his mother but then after receiving several tongue lashes I decided to back off and mind my own business. Besides, he had said this was the way he had always spoken to her since he was ten years old. Now raising a child in a place where communication was aggressive, my son just wet himself a lot when his dad was on the phone as most conversations would quickly escalate into a brawl. I would usually ask him to take the call in the bedroom, which he got offended asking *"How dare you tell me what to do?"*, so I would just walk away and keep the little boy in the room until the call was over.

FIRST TIME APART

I had been out of work and so money was tight, especially since we had invested in a lot of projects; music videos, a trip to the USA, and then he needed to give money to his parents too. We were down to nothing, literally living from hand to mouth, waiting on government benefits and vouchers for baby formula. I was pregnant yet my meals were restricted. I had some income from some online gigs and again I was hopeful that this could keep us going for a few months but it was at that same period that he needed to make a trip to Nigeria because he had dreamed that his dad was doing poorly. How could I even argue with that?

I could also have made a simple trip to Nigeria because I also wanted to meet his family and this would have been a good opportunity for them to meet our son. They seemed nice enough over the phone and I had absolutely no issues with them. All the stories he told me about them were questionable because they seemed pretty alright people in my opinion, but who was I to argue with his description of his own family. Anyways, it was decided that they were diabolic and it was not a good time for me since I was pregnant. To instill more fear in me he added that, Benin people could never be trusted, his mother's hands were not clean, and his brother's wife was two-faced. Now I was not going to go to Nigeria and die at the hands of Benin people! He also said we needed to manage our funds. This sounded pretty reasonable I thought.

Interestingly, this little trip ended up costing thousands. First of all were the outfits, everything had to be branded, so much spent on creating an impression. His brother had a house, they seemed close and so what was the point of lodging in a hotel? In his defense, he stated that he didn't trust his brother's wife. It seemed like whenever there was a bit of money, there was a financial need to be met that was not for us but someone else out there.

I kept telling him that we were giving people the impression that we had it all, but as usual, it fell on deaf ears. He was gone for a few days and in those days; I was instructed not to leave the house. He used to call at random times and insist on a video call just to ensure that I did not leave the house. He had managed to put this fear of the unknown in me that even in his absence I did not leave the house. I had this fear that if I went out to the playground, I would bump into one of the neighbours, and when he was back they would mention it in passing. Other paranoiac thoughts crossed my mind, like what if I fell down the stairs, what if my son ran off and I could not chase after him. This was the reality we lived in, and sadly it had begun to rub off on me, the fear of the unknown. I decided staying on the balcony was my best option; at least there was no way he would find out we were spending a lot of time there. In his absence, we had to manage with whatever food was available. It was difficult to smile at the fact that he was having a blast in Nigeria, eating whatever, buying things for people, splashing cash around, while my son and I had to make do and manage. And while he made me and the world believe that we were the most precious, the truth was; we were the least important because regular people would put a pregnant wife and child first.

SURVIVAL MODE ACTIVATED

With my experience of two prior pregnancies, I knew what to expect. Sadly, I was out of work, so it meant both of us, all day together and including a toddler. In my first pregnancy we were both at home and that pregnancy lasted only a few weeks. The second pregnancy I was at work until the week to birth, and I found my peace and chill zone at work. Now I was home and I was determined not to have history repeat itself. I mastered a way to zero my mind into a peaceful zone, keep calm regardless and try not to struggle during sex. Crossing the twelfth week was amazing, but every week, and every month came with new challenges. If it was not the arguments, it would be a screaming child, or money worries, or the sex.

I was sleep deprived most of the time and had to make out time to sleep day time. My son just could not sleep at night and would scream for no reason from about 11p.m until 3a.m and then just mysteriously fall asleep. I used to carry him, sing and rock him until he fell asleep. I had done this for two years plus. Now with a growing belly, it became more tasking. I could never have imagined that awkward sleep patterns in toddlers were one of the effects of being raised in an abusive house.

With all of this going on, sex could not be interrupted in anyway; his needs as a man had to be met whenever he needed it. It was either that or to listen to a speech of how I was frigid. Besides, I was fed up with being shouted at in front of my son, I had no intentions of having a son who would do the same to me or others. Just when I thought I had anticipated every form of pain, I did not know the worst was to come. I always questioned the way we had sex during pregnancy, it felt wrong, it felt dangerous, but I was done complaining. Besides, he would just remind me if it was not the same way we did it before. In fact I remember him saying uninformed things like *"The sex kept the baby healthy."*

Well now, it was about the eight month into pregnancy and all I had done was sit at home, no exercise, no walks, just sitting at home. My belly was obviously massively large; I had a few more weeks to my due date or a scheduled caesarean section. At eight months, the baby was already pressing seriously downwards against the uterus, sex was on the daily but what I was not expecting on that particular night was for him to stick his finger up my vagina. Now for a 6ft 3inch tall dude, I let you imagine how long his fingers are, including the fact that I usually had to beg to have his finger nails cut. While I was expecting the usual uncomfortable penis thrusts, I was not expecting that for the first time all he wanted was to finger me while jerking off. This did not make any sense; it was an unusual pattern to his advances. I screamed and squirmed in discomfort but he just kept saying,

"It's okay, I know what I'm doing, and I'm almost done".

He was done and I went to check myself because I was hurting a lot. I noticed that I was bleeding from my vagina. He called out to me saying there was blood on the sheets. In my mind I was expecting a bit of emotions, just a bit that says, *I'm sorry, I did wrong.* Instead all I got was,

"It's just stains, never mind". I was furiously angry. *"No way! We have to go to the doctor",* I insisted.

He was like

"But your water isn't broken so you're fine. Besides, its 3a.m in the morning, I really can't be bothered to go to the hospital now".

I was shocked, but also bothered because I knew having a baby survive until 8 months was not a guarantee that things could not go pear shaped. I sat up on the bed and watched him fall asleep. And about an hour later, he woke up and found me still sitting up and asked *"what's the problem?"* I said,

"We need to go to the hospital now; I need to know everything is okay". He agreed with a warning *"Better be careful about what you say because these people are always out to get an innocent man."*

Now at the time, I did not know this was abuse, or spousal rape, I just knew I was not happy, so no, I was not going to report abuse; I was just hoping someone would talk sense into him...into us. We got to the hospital and they ran some tests. Thankfully, the bleeding did not affect the baby, but the nurse said,

"Madam you need to stop having rough sex, your baby is almost due and this is not good at all."

I felt embarrassed because the choice of sex was not mine; the person in question was in the café having a snack when the message was delivered. I had never been so ashamed in all my life. I passed the message on to him in hopes that some of these behaviours would stop but it never did. The sex reduced but carried on at least 4 times a week. At that point I couldn't be bothered and I was up for whatever happened. I looked forward to my due date and those 2 days I would stay in the hospital without him. I remember chatting to a friend saying,

"I wish the U.K. was like America where I could stay in the hospital for up to a week after a caesarian section".

After some time in an abusive home, just like a soldier in a battlefield, your brain fortifies itself to deal with trauma and activates survival mode. You will spend much time coming up with strategies to survive and survival is all you will think about. The option of leaving will vaguely come to your mind. It's even worse when you haven't realised it is abuse. You latch on to the good times, and try to see how you can extend those good times even if it meant misery for yourself and your kids but that hope that never gets actualised.

Chapter 9

CHILD TWO- IT'S A GIRL!

O ur family was notorious for being late for everything, in fact in the first month of him securing a job; he was late most of the time. I was scheduled to have a caesarian section months in advance and we were well aware of the date and time. I was within hours of giving birth and I had no intentions of raising my Blood Pressure (BP). I had been on full compliance mode as I did not argue or contest anything. And as much as I was in disagreement with things, I learned to breathe and put my mind in a peaceful place. I came up with something called **"auto-pilot mode"** which meant, carrying on my day to day life without feelings or emotional attachment. What was most important was to bring forth this baby girl healthy and strong.

As usual, when I thought things could not get any worse, it did. On the day of birth was the day he decided to look for a child-minder. Apparently, he had not done it all this while as he had promised to do. It was the need to control and do everything that beat me. He would yell and say he was busy but why wouldn't he just let me find a child-minder myself? It was an app, it was quick and easy. He started on the day of my CS to search for nannies for my son; apparently he wanted the child-minder to come to the ward. I could not understand the motive behind this. We stayed in a lovely two bedroom flat, why could we not have a child-minder stay with our son in the flat for the few hours of my surgery. Well, all attempts failed, I kept reminding him that we needed to go to the hospital and he kept shutting me down. I was mad, but I remembered my blood pressure. I would not be allowed into theatre if there were any issues with my BP. *"Was he trying to trigger me intentionally?"* I thought. All the suggested options we could have used he turned down, like he had other options.

It was now time for my CS and we were still at home. The hospital had to ring asking if I was still attending my own CS. They actually made it clear that if I did not get there in the next half an hour they would have to cancel it. Now in the U.K. once you lose an appointment like that its going to be *a long thing (A Nigerian slang for "trouble")*. Remember this appointment was booked several months in advance. I pleaded with them that we were on our way and that there was a lot of traffic. Lies! We were still at home and had not even booked a cab. I felt my heart racing, and tears flowing down my cheeks, a glass of cold water would have been good to calm my nerves but I remembered I was not supposed to eat or drink. I went into the bedroom and muttered to myself,

"God help me keep calm."

I could literally feel my heart palpitations on my chest. I pulled myself together and went back to him and with a stern yet polite voice I said, *"Please call the cab, it will be terrible and possibly life threatening if I miss this appointment."*

We got to the hospital and the booking-in nurse was surprised. She had assumed the surgery was not going ahead because of the time we got there. She asked us to wait while she checked to see if the anesthesiologist and surgeons were still about and okay to go ahead. My heart was racing but my mind was also racing for ways to keep my heart chilled. I could not even begin to imagine how far this lackadaisical behaviour was going to go. Finally the nurse came and said they were set for me. We did not have a minder and I had to go in on my own because he had our son with him. I could not believe I was going into surgery on my own but I thought maybe it was a good thing, maybe with all the negativity, it was better this way; then another thought, what if anything happened no one would be there to hear my last words, but there's no way they were letting him into the theatre with a child.

It was awkward when the surgeon asked if I was doing this on my own. I had to answer all the questions and hope for the best. It was less turbulent and scary as the first CS. They brought her out and she did not cry, her eyes were wide open and she was staring at everyone. They cleaned her and gave her to me. The surgeon said my amniotic fluid was low. He said it was possible my waters had broken and I may not have realised it. He said it was a good thing we did not miss the appointment as it could have been detrimental to her. I was tired and was woozy, but I could not help thinking about all that rough and careless sex with all the positions. Within a few minutes of placing my daughter on my chest, she lifted her head up. This was shocking to everyone. I guess she was trying to tell me,

"I am the fight, I got you mum."

Each visit he made to the hospital was later than usual which made me wonder if there was any excitement on his part for the birth, *"aren't men supposed to be excited about daughters"*, I thought? I wished I could have stayed longer at the hospital. I did not want to go home. And then I returned home but what I met was not my expectation, there was no food for me to eat except this over peppery tasteless soup which I had rejected before I went into surgery two days before. I was just back from surgery and the only meal available was pounded yam. The pepper in that soup was not even good for me. As before, I had issues with blood clot and injections had to be given in my stomach. The house was a mess and it was heartbreaking that there were no preparations for me. I was unusually quiet and reserved, and to please me he arranged for my parents to visit. I was not excited about this. I remembered the last ordeal, what was the point of them buying their tickets to come down and be restricted from being with their grandchild/ children. Anyways, the arrangement had already been made. Maybe this time it could be better since he had a job and would not be around for at least 10 hours of the day. I was determined to give this baby a better start than what transpired with our son.

As usual, he had insisted on me not giving the baby a wash. This was a ridiculous ask in my opinion , because I was not going to do what we did before. Besides, he was working, and did not have time to give the kids a wash, so it meant the baby should be wiped until whenever he was available. Anyways, he was not home, so I gave her a wash and enjoyed mum and baby time with her and my son, and just lied to him that she had not had a wash. I remember him remarking about how clean she was and I just said I had done her daily wipes. It was nearly eight days after she was born that he was available to give her a wash. I watched him sit there giving instructions on how to wash a child while trying to hide my amusement. He insisted that he would give her a wash only on the weekends when he was free and I obliged because I knew once he left the house every Monday, I would be washing her as much as I wanted and doing all the things I never got to do with my son.

Interestingly, a victim is bent on ways to make things work in the midst of the chaos, this chaos isn't good for the kids, but we believe we can protect them.

MANIPULATION BY LIES

Things were basically as before; sadly the abnormal had become my normal. If there was any sort of interaction with other humans, other parents, families, just maybe he would see that this was not the way to live. But that was me not understanding the situation, I was not dealing with a person who would ever see reason, it had to be his way or the high way. I used to enjoy telephone conversations with his brother and his brother's wife. Our kids were about the same age so I looked forward to exchanging messages, pictures etc. Suddenly one day, he decided his brother's wife was a witch and responsible for the woes in their family, and he did not trust his brother not to pass pictures of our children to her. He said they were very jealous people. And just like that I was banned from chatting with them or exchanging messages. It was really terrible as my circle of people I could chat with over the phone was growing smaller by the day; the other thing was that this was his family and while I was banned from communicating with them, he carried on. And I kept complaining that he was giving them the wrong impression of me because all messages to his sisters and mum were restricted. I was not allowed to call them, I could only speak to them when he rang them and then beckoned on me to come say hello to them. He would hover around giving signals for me to limit conversations and round up after a few words. With all the things we had to argue about, I had no intention of adding fighting to speak to his family as one. I let him take the lead on how communication worked with them.

PARENTS ARRIVE

Like I said, I was determined to give this new baby a better start than my son but also catch up with things to do with him. It had been decided that I stayed home and not rush back to work, so that I mind the children. I did not oppose because I really needed to bond with my son, he was very distant. He seemed not to be clingy or cuddly like the usual 3 year olds, he only wanted to be carried when it was sleep time because he could not fall asleep without two hours of singing and rocking. It was almost like he felt no attachment to anything or anyone. He was also three years old and could not actually speak properly, according to his age chart. I felt like I could work on all these. Obviously, the isolation was a key impact and I hoped I could influence the decisions around keeping him at home all day.

Unbeknownst to me, that influence was not going to happen! He had left specific instructions that the kids should not be taken out of the house, in fact included that my dad was not allowed to carry the baby or touch her. He had this weird belief that my dad was going to infect the baby. Six months with my parents being around was a breather, we still had arguments but at least, when he was gone for those 10 hours, I got on with my mum and dad doing things the way I felt was best.

SHE'S DIFFERENT...SHE'S STRONG

Unlike my son, my daughter got to do belly time, crawl, I breastfed her as much as I pleased in his absence. She sat up at three months, babbled a lot and was very energetic. She had gorgeous hair and it never went patchy like my son's hair because she was never left in a baby seat all day or laying on her back. My mum and son accompanied me to all of my post natal checks, I ignored all the instructions he gave, and after all there was no way he would find out. We took long walks with my son and my daughter in the buggy. We stopped at the playground. I looked forward to every doctor's appointment because it was an opportunity to leave the house and take the kids with me outside, unlike in times past where my movements were quite limited. My mum could never understand why I would not just leave the house for walks or go to the city, go shopping and do normal things. My daughter was a warrior princess; she could not be subdued like my son. And that is probably because I was home and I allowed her a wiggle room to be normal within the confines of our abnormality.

Chapter 10

ABOUT CHILD ABUSE

Y ou may wonder why many women stay in abusive relationships? It is something that is difficult to explain, you will need to have walked the path to understand. You will also need an open and unbiased mind to take in some of the reasons. There are a few reasons but not exhaustive to why women stay in abuse; leaving in itself could be difficult. Abused Women see the person they fell in love with, the person that apologizes, the father of their children, while outsiders would see an abusive partner. Sometimes, abusers make it impossible for victims to leave. Victims are often isolated from friends and family and the world at large, there's no one to talk to about the abuse. Some abusers go as far as cutting off finance, internet, or even locking the victims at home. Meanwhile the victim has been in survival mode for a while and is just thinking about surviving and not escaping.

Women in abusive relationships need support and understanding not judgement. Sometimes women cry out about the abuse but the advice they receive is *"Stay for the children, pray, God hates divorce"* or *"Some people have had it worse but they stayed together, manage for a bit things will get better"* to mention a few. These sorts of advice and counsel should never be given to anyone going through abuse especially when children are involved. The truth is that beyond domestic violence, there is no real reason why anyone should stay in an unhappy place.

Did you know that when children are present in a household where domestic violence occurs, it is known as Child abuse? An estimated 90% of children whose mothers are abused witness the abuse. The effects are traumatic and long-lasting. An estimated 40% to 70% of these children are also direct victims of the abuse which takes place at home. An abusive partner = an abusive parent, this is not rocket science. It is who they are and their true nature will always turn up.

CHILD PROTECTION

Any harm done to a child is child abuse; harm includes treating children badly, making them ill, stopping them from growing or developing properly. My parents visited after the birth of my daughter and stayed for about six months. After they left, I got so bored staying at home. I had asked that my son be registered to start nursery with the September batch of 2016, he was three and half years old and ready. We argued about this and I backed down in agreement with him that the boy should stay at home until it was time for Infant School, in fact he said the boy shouldn't start school until he was five. I had two kids, stuck at home, and no money. I am very resourceful and creative; I can make something beautiful out of nothing, which probably is not just a blessing but a curse. I say this because all the times I tried to create a beautiful thing out of nothingness in that house, I shouldn't even have bothered. I requested for drawing sheets, pencils, and things like that because we had none of those at home. So, I used to look forward to going to Nando's and McDonald's so I could collect their crayons and colouring sheets to bring them home for my kids. He refused to buy writing materials, stating that my son would stab himself with them. I requested for a chalk board so my son could practice writing and drawing, but all of that was ignored...discarded. He wanted to control and subdue me, to make sure I did not have anything I wanted or made me happy, however the kids suffered for these actions. A full two months after my parents left, I stayed home with the kids, not leaving the house or anything, I got really fed up! Leaving my son at home for another year and half meant my never leaving the house as well. Besides, we were not actively learning or doing anything, so what was the point of keeping him at home.

At about two years and ten months, I noticed that my son had started regressing. This was the same boy that had passed his two and half year doctors check but now a year later, he could neither hold a spoon, nor could he speak, he just wanted to point at things rather than speak. It took a lot to convince my ex to get my son a toddler's high chair. I thought a high chair and tray would help him learn to feed himself and have hand-eye coordination but my ex would always come up with extreme cases, of the child choking to death, going blind because he put food in his eyes. I was like but the boy is approaching four years. He would snap at me asking how busy I was that I could not feed my son,

"Oh I bet you want to leave him on the high chair so you can go on your phone." He would say. This right here is also child abuse. Not allowing a child develop.

In my ex's mind, everything was hazardous, toys were too heavy, *"He could kill his sister with it",* and so we locked away all toys except soft toys. Then I negotiated for "**One toy a week**" I just did not understand why the children were not allowed to just thrive. Sometimes I would just rebel and bring out toys for them, after all he was not home, and then put them away before he got back. My son got a trike as a birthday present from the Pastors. They must have thought we would have found it very useful because we had several play areas where we lived. Well, that trike only left the house once after I begged repeatedly. I ended up wheeling my son on it around the house; he loved it so much to the extent that it was used for his meal times (this was before we got the high chair). I could never understand why we could not just take the trike out and push the boy around and let him play. My ex was also anti- scooters and anti-bicycles, which is why my children never had any. He said it was too dangerous.

We fought about my son going to nursery until he gave in towards the end of September and I got my son registered; it was free by the way. With all excitement, I was like *"Yes!"* Only for him to come back and say he'd changed his mind, a day to when my son was to start. My heart broke. He had a long list of reasons, and I had to call the school to say we were not ready yet. You see, at all times I had to have his approval to do things because he had put this paranoid fear in me that if I did anything he wasn't in agreement with, something bad was going to happen and over time I believed it. Please do not underestimate the power of brainwashing, cults, top military institutions and extremists use it. It's the same with domestic violence.

We fought some more about the school because it was October, he said, *"Alright go ahead"*, and then few days to start, he declined again. The next reason was that he had to travel for his dad's burial so I needed to wait till he got back. Now there was no sense in it because he was traveling in November to be back in December a few weeks to the Christmas break, which would mean that the boy would attend nursery for two weeks and then the long Christmas break. I refused; I knew he did not want me leaving the house while he was in Nigeria nothing more.

An abuser does not care about the welfare of the children, so do not be deceived by their dramatic show of concern. We fought more about the nursery and I went into a very obvious mode of depression. My face was expressionless, I did not laugh, and I spoke only when spoken to in a very low tone and no eye contact. After a few weeks, he agreed for him to be registered yet again. I told him that if I registered our son this time, I was not going back to say we are not ready or make excuses about my son being unwell." Sadly, when I went back to the school, it was a few days to the October half term holidays and they said I would need to start in November. You can see how a simple thing as a three and half year old boy going to nursery dragged for nearly two months.

I anticipated November and the little lad started nursery. My ex made me call him off school for the littlest things like a cough, a rash, he looks tired etc. But going to nursery brought about some discoveries. On the first day of nursery my son walked into the classroom and did not look back to say *"Bye mummy"* no emotions, no crying, no tears, nothing! When I got back to pick him up at closing, he did not want to leave the classroom. It was a lot of effort for them to bring him out. I thought that was strange. Here was a child that had been at home for a year and half, I would have thought he would have been eager to come home.

But then again I noticed that at nursery there were toys, it was relaxing, and he could enjoy himself doing all the kiddie activities, meanwhile at home the kids were restricted to toys they had access to. And while I felt like he should have missed me for being away from him for 3 hours, for the first time in over 2 years, I was happy at least that my son was in school. My son in nursery was the beginning of a new chapter that none of us was expecting not even me and I spoke about this in the earlier chapters of this book, *"Violence, sex and the fetus"* even before they are born. When my son was in nursery, the teachers picked up on the fact that he was comfortable staying in the corner, not interacting with any children- he found himself a piece of paper and would just make senseless scribbles on the paper, inappropriate play with toys, usually just slamming or trying to reap them apart or if he found himself a calculator where he just punched numbers on it all day and he wouldn't move. He would stand in the corner pressing those numbers until he wet himself and he would not want to be changed, he was comfortable to stay in his wet knickers. Now I had mentioned my concerns about my son slamming and ripping things apart in a destructive manner, but papa bear said it was normal and he too was like that as a child.

Initially the nursery put my son's lack of communication and interaction down to the fact that he had not be around other children but as time passed and not much progress was being made in the areas of his speech and social interactions, an educational psychologist and speech therapist were employed to work with him. Also referrals were populated to the pediatrics team. The referrals came through and my ex had no interest in following through with them claiming the boy was fine and there was nothing wrong with him. About six months before my son started nursery, a friend had seen my son and sent a message saying his behaviours were similar to a child on the ASD spectrum. My ex was furious and in fact insisted we cut off from that person. Now with the nursery mentioning the same thing, I was insistent that we sort help for our child. I didn't know much about autism but if it was a term constantly flying around, I saw no reason why we shouldn't look into it. We missed the first paediatric appointment for a flimsy reason. Truth is he just didn't want to attend. I rebooked the appointment again, (bearing in mind that there are long waiting lists to get an appointment) I kid you not, after months of waiting for the appointment date for the paediatrician; we got to the appointment 50 minutes late. Remember, our family had formed the habit of being late, even worse when it was something he wasn't interested in. Not much could be achieved on the day so we had to be rebooked again for another appointment. By the time we finally got to see the paediatrician, my son had finished the year in nursery and was now in reception. On the day of the appointment there was war! He kept arguing with the doctor and contesting every point. And the doctor kept saying, *"No one says your son is autistic, but several referrals have been put forward indicating concerns about patterns of behaviour"* Again I could not imagine that he would neglect an opportunity to better our son's condition. This is undoubtedly child abuse.

Another notable incident about nursery was the requirement to have the child potty trained before start date as diapers were not allowed. I had to do this within a couple of months before he started. As I started potty training, his dad showed no interest, he would not render any assistance in potty training, saying there was no need that humans would naturally learn to go to the toilet on their own when the time was right. I had to start potty training him and, it was a nightmare. It was confusing for him that I would sit to *do a wee,* and then I wanted him to stand. I tried to get his dad to show him, but he blatantly refused.

Besides my son did not recognise the urge to want to go to the bathroom, remember that when mum and dad argued, he'd wet himself and I wasn't allowed to change him immediately, so he grew used to having a wet bottom. Since his dad would not teach him, I had to devise a means to it; I was constantly looking for a way to make a way where there was no way. I came up with a strategy to use a washing up liquid can (Fairy ©brand) to teach my son. I would put it between my legs and squeeze, so he could understand that that is what he was expected to do. I did that several times over but he just was not getting it.

The issue was he had developed a habit of being comfortable in his mess. All those times when he would wet himself or poo accidentally, and his dad would prevent me from changing his Pampers©, my son was actually comfortable staying that way. I did not realise the impact of domestic violence on my children. Finally one day, miraculously, my son was in the bedroom and shouted *"mummy wee wee wee wee wee wee"*, I rushed to the bedroom, jubilating that *"He's got it right",* I asked if he wanted to do wee but he shook his head and was pointing at the television. I found it hilarious that he was referring to an advert that came up on TV and the advert was the Fairy washing up liquid. I think he had looked at it and he related that advert to the fact that I always had a washing up liquid bottle and I said *"wee wee wee"* as well, eventually my son got potty trained. However, whenever he was in nursery he just wet himself uncontrollably and he was happy to stay wet.

I did not at the time know that one of the symptoms of child abuse is, wetting themselves. Not only did my son not understand the sensation that prompts the need for easing himself, he did not understand hunger, thirst, and tiredness to mention a few. You see, when he ate, he had to be reminded to swallow and drink some fluids otherwise he'd keep stuffing his mouth until he choked. If he was thirsty, he would not ask for a drink, or go get a drink. I would have to mentally work out when he needed any of these.

Neglecting a child is another massive area in child abuse that goes unnoticed. People may only look at the extremes of neglect, but neglect includes ongoing failure to meet a child's basic physical or emotional needs, failure to provide adequate food, clothing and shelter for children as well as failure to protect them from physical, emotional harm or even danger; this includes during pregnancy.

My daughter was hitting two and half years old and it was the same pattern, not allowed to go to play clubs or child activities. In fact at the time, our neighbour had a 3 year old daughter and it would have been a perfect friendship, but remember we were not allowed to interact with the world. My movements were monitored more than ever, because he did not trust my son being in school, so I had to text before I left the house, and when I got back. If there were any delays or variations in my timings, he would instantly start a video call to verify where I was. One time I had a parent feedback meeting in school and he video called me during the meeting just to verify my location.

At times, all I thought about was, at least my son was in school, and for 6 hours he would have a normal life. My daughter and I got up to all kinds of things. While he insisted that she was left in the buggy like my son, I used to let her walk to school without his knowledge, I would let her pick up leaves and enjoy nature within the confines of the timings. My son was hyper-sensitive to textures because he was never allowed messy play.

I tried everything to avoid being screamed at before the kids. We had instances, when he was shouting and my son began to kick him, another instance my daughter would yell, *"Shut up!"* And though it felt like they were trying to protect me, I thought it was not right, I should protect them. When my daughter spoke, she spoke with authority, like she was giving orders, but of course, that was all she was used to. She was growing and maturing faster than my son who was three years older. She was also physically stronger. While my daughter could hold a pen tripod way, it took my son until he was nearly six years old to do the same. It was not his fault; he was not allowed to develop properly.

After my daughter clocked two years old, I watched my ever chatting girl, who used to try to talk to everyone on the streets during school runs, begin to act overly shy, run away from people, and refusing to chat. She began to regress, not wanting to socialise or speak; she would rather just point at things as opposed to using her words.

My heart sank, *"That was what happened to my son at about the same age and now we are dealing with autism"* I thought and I blamed it all on lack of interaction, even though now I know it was way beyond that. I began to put pressure on him about letting me take her to play groups, since he said nursery was out of the question and she was too young. I suggested, parks and event for kids, but he refused, stating that we were going to repeat the same method we used for our son. I got fed up with asking.

I tried my best to make sure she had as many activities in the house, tried to get her writing, colouring, browsed YouTube to get ideas on programs that would be helpful for her learning in general. And because I was not actually interacting with anybody, the child was not interacting as well. She got really comfortable talking to me, we would talk forever but she would not speak to anyone else. When I went for school runs for my son, I had a limited time to say *hello* to people and take off back home, before my movements were questioned. Sometimes I tried to go 1 or 2 minutes earlier for school runs so that maybe we could catch up with some other mums, ask questions but then I would be questioned on why I was leaving early. Sometimes,

I would delay my return home by a few minutes and come up with a lie that I had to talk to the teacher just so I could spend some more time with the other mothers and that is what life was like generally. So my daughter stayed home without externally developmental or stimulating activities.

Finally, it was time for her two and half year check with the health visitor, the health visitors interestingly picked up on a few things. She said,

"Your child has good eye contact, good writing skills, a good hand grip and hand to mouth movement but I have noticed that she is struggling with interactions." All through the visit my daughter did not say a word to anybody she did not speak to anyone, did not react or show interest in the other kids. It was at that point the health visitor asked if she could talk. I tried to get her to at least talk, or make a sound but all attempts were futile. I had to show them a recorded video of my daughter talking in the house. At that point, they asked,

"Does she go to playgroup or nursery? Does she go to the play centre?" Does she go to any children's centre activities or mum and baby groups?"

My response was *"No"* to all the questions.

Then they asked if I was planning to enroll her in nursery and I told them that that would happen when she would clock 4 years of age. Their verdict was

"What is going on here is that your child is not used to humans except those at home, she's not used to interacting with others and has no understanding of the world."

They advised that nursery was free, and the activities at the play centers and children's centers were free, that I needed to start involving her, but what they did not know was my situation at home, otherwise they would have flagged up not just domestic violence but child abuse. Not allowing your child access age appropriate and developmental activities is Child Abuse.

I took all the information and leaflets home, hopeful that this would create a change in my ex's thought process. Again, my hopes were dashed. I knew it was more about me not interacting but there were activities on the weekends, there were also dad and baby activities which I said he if he could take her since he did not want me going, but he said he was too busy and tired on the weekend. Just so you know, our weekend activities were to argue through Friday night, end with makeup sex, wake up Saturday very late, well even if I was awake, we had to wait for when he was ready to get out of bed, Sunday, stay home, watch movies. So asked me again, what was so busy about the weekend? Yet he said,

"The child is too young and she's not going anywhere"

Then I got really upset and stated the obvious,

"She's becoming like her brother" I blurted out, *"She's not speaking any more, she's scared of people when they try to say*

hello, she now tippy toes and flaps like him and would rather point to things than speak"

Our son was on a referral pathway for Autism and I made it quite clear that it was his fault for not letting the boy interact and now, we could have a daughter with the same challenges. He snapped at me saying,

"There was nothing wrong with our son, he will outgrow it"

He also stated that our daughter was spiritual and was able to see the negative energies of people which was why she ran away. Also said,

"I do not talk to other people's children, why should they talk to my child."

Then he switched everything and said I was to blame for whatever was going on with my children, I was a terrible mother and that was why I kept looking for the easy way out of having others look after my kids.

On several occasions our son was neglected because the ex just had this whole thing of being in control and not letting anyone touch the child. I remember once we bumped into an old acquaintance at the train station and he was shocked we had a child. You see, only a select few knew about the existence of our children, and only direct family and maybe one or two friends were allowed to see pictures of them. He would always remind me that nobody saw the faces of Michael Jackson's children until he died, so this was nothing new. Furthermore, the schools were not allowed to take pictures or videos of our kids. I remember thinking if this was the same person that before marriage had told me, when we had kids in the future, he'd love them to be models. Anyways, the old acquaintance asked for the name of our son and before I could respond, he blurted out,

"His name is Titus."

I was in utter shock but played along, that was not the name of our son! Later on he explained that he had to do that because we could not trust people with the name of your child. Imagine growing up and having your dad introduce you with fake names every time...how confusing that would be for a child?

Each time we had to shoot a music video or performance at a musical concert, he would insist on bringing the child. Some of these video shoots lasted 6 to 8hours. In that time he would insist that the child minder should not bring the boy out of the car seat. Some of the events we attended were night programs, from 8pm till 1 am; there was really no reason to bring a one year old along. This is child abuse now these are the things that I suffered because my life was quite controlled and as a result, these sorts of behaviours were transmitted to the children. I was at the time on survival mode; I did not realise like most people, that the impact of domestic violence is very dire on the children, you do not want to stay in an abusive relationship you want to get out of that relationship even if not for yourself but for your children.

My son was hypersensitive to loud noises, and would scream uncontrollably in church, or even at his 1st birthday when the kids shouted *"Happy Birthday"* in unison. All that continued until he was well over five years old. Not allowing the boy walk when he could walk was also neglect. I argued about it but then I gave up arguing and choose my peace but if I had any clue that the impact on the children was going to be potentially long lasting, I probably would have kicked harder against it. This is why I'm writing this book so that if you are in a similar situation saying *"I will find a way to make peace in the home, I will find a way to make the normal out of the abnormal"* Trust me I did all that while unknowingly subjecting my children to unnecessary suffering, health issues and child abuse.

PHYSICAL ABUSE (CHILD ABUSE)

Physical abuse in children is one that we all have high signals for. A child should not witness physical violence! I remember once being slapped hard on my back while I was breastfeeding my two months old daughter, and in front of my son. It was almost midnight and we were conversing, he asked a question, I responded and then I got a slap. I was shocked, it was incomprehensible and he defended it while shouting on top of his voice. My son was there staring, and playing with his fingers. I put my daughter in her cot and walked away to the living room.

Physical abuse also includes not only deliberately hurting or harming a child, it includes making them ill, hitting or shaking a child. Evidently, you will find that in many homes, physically abusive parents insist that their actions are simply forms of discipline—ways to make children behave. But there is a big difference between using physical punishment to discipline and physical abuse. Whether physical harm is deliberate or indeliberate, it is still child abuse.

Just like adult victims of abuse have to walk about on egg shells, the same goes for their children. Abusers are unpredictable and so the child never knows what is going to set the parent off. There are no clear boundaries or rules, which leaves the child never sure what behaviour will trigger a physical assault. There was an instance where my ex was telling me off and my son was mucking about, making noise and just out of the blues, his dad gave him a hot slap which threw the boy right across the bed and he slammed his head on the wall creating massive goose bumps. I was shocked because this was the same person that seemed to dote over the boy and let him have his way with everything. I remember the shocked look on my son's face; I do not think he ever imagined that. I held him and cuddled him as he screamed his guts out.

OUTBURST OF ANGER

Abusive parents act out of anger and the desire to assert control and not the motivation to lovingly teach the child. The more anger in the parent, the more intense the abuse. They use fear to control behaviours. Abusive parents may believe that their children need to fear them in order to behave, so they use physical abuse to *"Keep their child/ children in line."* However, what children are really learning is how to avoid being hit, not how to behave or grow as individuals.

Staying in that marriage and in that abusive home was indeed child abuse and detrimental to my kids. Remember that in an abusive home, there is only one reasonable person and that person is the victim. The abuser will abuse the child in proxy as they abuse their victim. There were countless instances of my ex lashing out in anger towards the kids because he could not stand their noise. He would say things like,

"Get out of here! Look at them acting like little demons!"

I cautioned him but he justified it by saying the kids had no clue, after all he was speaking pidgin English but I insisted that regardless of whether they understood or not, the words did not just sound pleasant. He would snap at them for touching his work table at home, his pillow, his shoes, and every little thing would set him off. If we ever went out for a meal and the kids started crying or something, or doing what normal children do, playing with stuff on the table or touch the table that would set him off. All of this was way before Covid-19 yet there I was being made to sanitize the surfaces before we could sit for a meal. If either of the children touched anything outside the sanitized areas, he was going to blow a fuse. This is child abuse; do not wait for your child to get hit.

WITNESSING SEXUAL VIOLENCE (CHILD ABUSE)

When we had one child we lived in a two bedroom flat, the second room was empty, yet he would insist on having sex with my son in the room, sometimes my son would wake up and crawl into our bed yet he would still carry on. Remember, half the time, our sex was not *"normal"* sex; it involved tears, *"tears"* and blood. When we had two children, we lived in a three bedroom house, yet both kids stayed in the same room with us, my daughter, in a cot bed and, my son on our bed. I suggested several times, that we could go to the other room, or to the living room, but he always declined, maintaining that it was a *"quickie"* which was a lie and half the time our son would wake up.

INAPPROPRIATE BEHAVIOURS.

While I cannot judge anyone for how they run their homes, I personally never saw my mum or dad walking about naked in the house and I saw no reason why he did that. He used to get mad that I would cover up after a wash especially in front of the children; then we would have a huge argument that I was hiding myself from him because I had a mystery boyfriend. However, I made it clear that I found it inappropriate to be jingling my bits in front of a five year old boy or him in front of a two year old girl.

Remember that while some children may overcome the physical and psychological effects of child abuse, particularly those with strong social support and resiliency skills, they can adapt and cope with bad experiences, many others may result in physical, behavioural, emotional or mental health issues even years later, this is my story, and I hope it will not be yours after you read this book. Choose right, do right.

Chapter 11

TIME TO GO

A fter over seven years of being in an endless cycle, constantly being told that we can start all over with a series of , *"I'm sorry, it would not happen again, I'll change this and that, in a while, when the kids are a bit older, I'll let you take them out".*

There was always one reason or the other or one promise of a brighter future, sadly that future never seemed to come.

My son was now over five years old, and my daughter over two years old nothing had changed. The year 2017 winter had an amazing outpour of snow; everyone in the Streets' Close with children came out to play. We were not allowed to go out in the snow, with a long list of improbable reasons such as , *"They will catch a cold, they will fall over"* etc, and so my kids stayed at the window watching other kids play snowballs, sledge, giggle and just have fun. Imagine being a Frozen© fan, and then see snow, but cannot touch it or experience it.

The snow stayed for three days from Friday to Monday after he went to work, I took them to the back of the house and we built a snow man together. When he came back I lied that it was just me, and that the kids watched from the window. The good thing was that there was no way for him to prove otherwise, my son could not express himself, and my daughter was no longer interested in talking.

He would buy toys, and then if one child was to slam it on the floor, he would lock it away claiming that it was hazardous. It was getting challenging trying to create a normal life for the kids with fewer resources. For those that haven't experienced domestic violence, you might wonder, with all this going on, why don't women leave? First off, we need to stop blaming victims for staying and start supporting them to enable them to leave because there are many barriers that stand in the way of a woman leaving an abusive relationship and these could be psychological, emotional, financial, or physical threats. Let us normalise supporting and empowering women to make the best decision for themselves while holding abusers solely accountable for their behaviour. There's a long but not exhaustive list of reasons. One of the questions we hear repeatedly is *"Why didn't/doesn't she just leave?"*

Danger and fear are two of the many reasons women do not leave, it can be incredibly dangerous. The fear that women feel is very real and there is a huge rise in the likelihood of violence after separation. Roughly 41% (37 of 91) of women are killed by a male partner/former partner in England,

Wales and Northern Ireland yearly (Annual Report on UK Femicides 2018 www.femicidecensus.org) and the numbers are on the rise. This takes place when they had separated or taken steps to separate from them. Eleven of these 37 women were killed within the first month of separation and 24 were killed within the first year.

Isolation is the breeding ground of abuse, the perpetrator works to weaken the women's connections with family and friends, making it extremely difficult to seek support. Perpetrators will often try and reduce a woman's contact with the outside world to prevent her from recognising that his behaviour is abusive and wrong. A lot of women are in abusive relationships and do not even know. Isolation leads women to become extremely dependent on their controlling partner.

There is also the element of shame, embarrassment and /or denial. Perpetrators are often well respected or liked in their communities because they are charming and manipulative. This prevents people from recognising the abuse. The perpetrator often puts down, denies or inculpates the abuse on the victim. Victims may be ashamed or make excuses to themselves and others to cover up the abuse. The lack of credence, as well as the trauma of being told daily that you are trashy will have a negative impact on your self-assurance. Victims have very restricted freedom to make decisions in an abusive relationship, they are often traumatized, regularly told that they need the perpetrator and could never survive on their own. Fear is constant and they live in a world of everyday terror.

Other reasons include the fact that abusers often control every aspect of their victim's life, making it impossible to gain economic self-sufficiency. By controlling access to money women are left unable to support themselves or their children. They may fear having their children taken away or even that the abuser may harm the children. Support isn't always readily available and in fact a lot of times when they ask, they may get the wrong advice or the person get around to telling the abuser and that gets them in more trouble.

There's also anxiety, depression, trauma and PTSD, all of this makes a person unable to make the right choices. The truth is many victims are walking corpses; they just exist but have actually given up. Let us not forget trauma bonding, codependency and Stockholm syndrome.

In my case, every attempt to get the kids engaged in social activities failed, I was stuck trying to create social activities in the house. I had to be creative to make sure the kids were not missing. For instance when they were not allowed to go outside and play when it snowed, I got fluff from a pillow, threw it up and shouted snow. One time we bought some beds for the kids that came in big massive cartons, I had asked him if I could turn them into play houses for the kids but he said it was unsafe...everything was unsafe in his mind. He wanted us to stay isolated, and be bitter at the world, for him everyone was bad, and people were after us and we had to be protected from them. Most times, after he left for work, I did my own thing and made two massive play houses for the kids, and we did everything from cops and robbers, to hide and seek, until we were exhausted. Just before he came back, I packed up the cartons and put them outside for collection. It was heartbreaking to see my kids cry because they could not understand why I got rid of the cartons. I used to do laundry quite often just so there would be a reason to go to the back garden and take the kids along. We were prohibited from going to the garden; he would make random video calls just to verify that we were not outside. He would inspect them on return for signs of dirt, a tan, or check their shoes or mine, to confirm that we were not outdoors.

Now the reason we moved to a big house which was ridiculously expensive was because he said if we had a garden, we would install swings, and slides for the kids. I believed as usual, but a year and half later, no outdoor toys or equipment in the garden, in fact we were not even allowed to go in the garden because he believed there was someone watching me. My kids were interested in the ice cream van; my daughter had never had that experience. My son had once but I never spoke about it because he would have been mad. I got my kids ice cream, just so they could have that experience of running to the ice cream van and ordering some. I made them stand on a spot at the back of the house to have it. When they were done, I had to clean off all evidence, from the house all the way to the street where we got the ice-cream. Every single drop of ice cream that would attract ants, I wiped clean, I changed the kid's clothes, washed/dried them, and put them back on. This was where all the knowledge from watching crime scene movies came in handy. My kids could not communicate, so I knew that even if he asked them a hundred times about their day, they would not be able to say anything. His issue with the ice-cream vans was that he said that it was made by Asians and he had had a dream that the Asians in the U.K. were planning to take over by poisoning everyone. One time, he got home and my daughter started chanting "Ice-cream, ice-cream" and he asked if I had taken them for ice cream, I just lied that it was from a YouTube video. I quickly played an ice-cream video for him to show evidence. I did not realise that my kids were watching me, even though they could not communicate, even though they could not talk, they were watching me so tensely trying to hide things and delete evidence. This was also imprinting fear in their hearts. It was also very exhausting to come up with a cover up and counter story for trying to live a normal life.

With time, when he came home from work and began to shout about something or anything, the kids would begin to protest in their own way; screaming, banging toys, throwing stuff. He could not bear the noise or screams, and would snap and walk away complaining. You see, when he was out, it was different, the house was calm and quiet, with coordinated noise but when he was in, it was war with the kids. It was good to have them distract him from his circular conversations but then I thought it was not their job to protect me but the other way round. Sometimes, my daughter would shout, *"Shut up, stop shouting"* while my son would kick him. It was getting out of hand.

BACK TO WORK...ON REPEAT!

Again we were evicted for the fourth time in six years of marriage and within a year from our previous eviction. This time, it was going to be difficult to secure a new place on his salary; we needed to be both income earners. I seized that opportunity to suggest I went back to work. Do not forget I was and still am a money making machine, I could easily make his full month's wages in less than ten days. There was no real reason for keeping me at home for 3 years while we struggled financially. He agreed to the idea with a long list of terms and conditions which fell on deaf ears (his terms and conditions made me smile) as long as it meant my going back to work. I got a job offer within a few weeks and that opened another can of worms.

Since I was going back to work, we needed a child minder for the kids. I suggested it was the best time to put our girl in nursery and then a child minder for the rest of the hours. But he refused, I was compelled to reject my job offer but then we couldn't secure a house and so I had to go back again to ask if they would still have me but with a different start date which was to be the beginning of the summer break. All this happened because he said he could not trust a child minder doing school runs. He wanted a child minder that would stay at home with the kids and not leave the house. He always made it clear that he did not trust me with the kids but now he said he trusted me over a child minder whose profession was to manage kids?

This was an impossible ask because I knew no **normal** person would do what I did for years. We struggled to get a nanny as anyone that indicated interest, he would turn them down. One time, when I thought I had found the perfect person, the kids were a bit noisy and as a result he rejected her saying, *"The children are reacting to the bad energy of the person."*

There was this one nanny who, in my opinion, would have been every parent's dream, this lady was promising stuff like taking the children to the zoo, play centres, library for activities. This was my dream, having the kids attend social activities, plus she had a son about the same age as my daughter, so it was perfect, they would have an additional friend. He rejected her saying his kids were not to leave the house. I remember her saying,

"You are a super mum; I do not know how you have raised these lovely, intelligent children without human interaction". She went further to say that an understanding of the world and environment was a key part of a child's development. She also remarked that our house looked like we had no kids, no toys laying about, nothing in the garden, no writing materials, and said she was happy to bring some. After she

left, he blew up, saying in fact I should forget the job and stay home.

We finally secured a nanny, who was willing to start at the beginning of the summer holidays which was perfect. She unwillingly agreed to our terms and conditions of staying indoors, it was obvious by every facial expression that it did not make sense but I believe she needed the money. She started and I was off to work. On her first day, when I returned home, I noticed she looked really red and unwell, I asked if she was okay and she said, she felt really sick staying at home all day, that it was hot and not airy. She pleaded to take them out, but I declined. I was under *"Authority"* and I did not want to start anything that would make him insist I leave my job.

Another unnerving thing was that in our house, the curtains were always drawn; the house was not really well lit with sunlight because he had always alleged that people were looking into the house. The health visitor that visited when my son was born had also remarked that we needed to let bright light into the house and a bit of fresh air. I came home and noticed she had opened the curtains and the windows. I knew if he saw this, all hell would break loose. I needed to give her a bit of leeway, so she would not quit, so I did not stop her from opening the curtains or window. What I did was as soon as she left I would shut everything in order for him not to find out: even at that he still had his suspicions because the curtains looked like they had been touched. The nanny was amazing; I allowed her do whatever she deemed fit within the confines of our house, just to keep her sweet. There was a lot I hid from him, like she sat in the garden with the kids, they had picnics at the back, she baked and cooked with them, also brought writing materials for them. In a normal home, these things were not bad, but in ours it was a taboo, so I had to hide it from him.

Her tenure ended but I still needed more time since I could not get anyone else, she gave one condition that would guarantee her return and that was that she would be allowed to take the kids out. He refused and threatened that I would have to quit my job if I could not find anyone, afterall family always comes first. I was stuck and the only option was to ask for 1 week's annual leave, even though I had only started the job 3 weeks back. Luckily, they were understanding and agreed. In that week, I tried my best to get a nanny to no avail, I suggested nursery for my daughter, and he still declined! And for the first, I snapped. I found some nurseries nearby, went to them with the kids in his absence, picked one and registered my daughter. I also got after school care for my son. I paid for these once my salary hit my account, before he could see it and withdraw the money. In fact my daughter started her nursery settling in period while I was on annual leave without his knowledge.

Two days to my planned return to work, I summoned the courage and told him, I had registered her. I had never been so scared and bold at the same time. There was nothing he did not say, raging, swinging his hands as he spoke, and I stood there asserting that I was not going to cancel her registration and she goes to school. We battled the matter that weekend, the kids were terrified but I put my foot down. You may be wondering, where did my unusual strength come from? It came from coming out of isolation. My change was because for the first time I had access to a computer so I could research things at work without his knowledge. I had mixed up with other humans, and I got loads of validation at work, I began to remember who I was. My standing up to him for the first time unraveled him and he became a ticking time bomb. I saw sides of him I had not seen in over seven years of marriage. He began to ring people, telling them his marriage was over; his wife was out of control and would not listen, to some he cried over the phone. A week after my daughter began nursery, he came home and said, he was going to end it all since I do not need him, he was going to go out there and not return, he would put something in his drink. All of this was shocking to me but I still insisted I was not quitting the job, or pulling her out of school. I suggested a mediator, and for the first time he obliged.

I really needed someone to listen to us speak individually because I could not make sense out of anything, I did not know who was right or wrong plus I felt guilty for putting my daughter in nursery without telling him. It was the first time in a long time I was taking a decision without him or against his wish and he was good at making me feel guilty. The lady he invited came and listened to him speak, it was the first time she was ever meeting him in person, I did not even have a clue who she was... she mentioned domestic violence. She told us that she was under the impression that our girl was a baby, but now seeing she was nearly three and never been anywhere, the story changed, and not to his favour. He struggled to keep calm, tapping his foot, standing and sitting, adjusting his belt. He was struggling not to explode. In all that drama, I fixed my eyes on the mediator, I noticed how she was watching him. She left after a few hours and advised him to calm down and stop being over anxious and let his children thrive. As soon as she left, he blew up, demanding that I had to take our daughter out of school. I refused with the strong reason that the mediator whom he brought, said I should not and that got him really mad. Our relationship was weird, but every single opportunity I had, I studied more on the topic of domestic violence. Now my eyes had been opened to the topic by the mediator. The more I studied, the more my heart bled. I did not realise this was what I was dealing with. It was saddening because I realised I had wasted over 7 years of my life hoping for a change that would never come.

Every survey or anonymous chat I engaged with came up with *"You need to get out, your life is in danger"* I did not know where to start or what to do. Was it really over? Surely there could be a way. After all I had won a few battles, being back at work, having my daughter in school, so maybe things could progress if I kept standing my ground.

ANOTHER HELLISH HOLIDAY

We carried on like cat and dog, and I just kept trying to change things, but it was hell to keep living like that especially since I now knew what I was dealing with. I slept in fear of the unknown, thinking every night I closed my eyes could be my last. He got more verbally abusive but there was nothing I had not heard before so I cared less. I could see he was unraveling, I could see it worried him that I was not as compliant as before. So he decided to win me over with a family trip for Christmas. I suggested we go see his family in Europe or a few other places but he said no. He wanted to go back to America which was expensive and unaffordable. We had to use all of my salary and credit card just to make this trip. I suggested alternative locations and different flights, but he insisted as usual to use the most expensive route. I had told myself that this trip would be the last opportunity to save the marriage.

The house we stayed in had 6 adults and 3 children; most were relatives which meant that even if we did not go anywhere my kids were in a place where they saw so many people. I watched my children, my daughter especially run away when folks tried to approach her. She struggled to interact with both adults and kids. My son was a bit sociable yet communication was a struggle for him. The events that transpired in those three weeks' holiday, made me realise that if I indeed made it back to the United Kingdom alive, we had to run!

It all started when we arrived there to find a male family friend also lodged there in the basement, he decided instantly that there was something going on between myself and the fella. Another time he accused the man of trying to use some voodoo on me. Now this was a married man with a family based in the USA, why would he want me from the UK with two children? As a result, he got really verbally abusive, more sexual assaults, and threatened on several occasions, in his words,

"I'm ready to end it all and when I'm done; your family can call the police."

Now these words sent chills down my spine and put much fear in me especially because I had read a lot on the internet, so I knew for a fact that they were beyond words. I made a painful decision to comply with everything he wanted, with the hopes that that could keep me safe until we got back to the U.K. While on holiday, we were banned from interacting in his absence, he had to follow me and the kids everywhere. We were not allowed to leave the bedroom, until he was ready to go down himself. The kids usually got up at 6 a.m while their dad slept until 10a.m, then took his time to have a wash and dress up and went down at about midday; so until midday, we all stayed hungry. I asked often if the kids could go ahead and have breakfast with the other kids but he refused claiming that a mother and father must be with their kids and that that man may poison them. It was heartbreaking, when my son would say things like, *"Mummy and daddy are talking again."* I tried to use the fact that we were in the midst of people to push certain boundaries to the advantage of the children, but I would get a signal or a text to come up stairs, and he would boil over in rage. One time he was angry and started the usual 4 hours circular conversation, and by the time he was done, my daughter had fallen asleep, she missed lunch. Sexual violence escalated, we hardly slept at night because arguments carried on well into 3a.m in the morning. Everything around me felt like it was going to be my last days, and I began to prepare by sending out emails through my work email, the one place he did not have access to. Sadly, those that received the messages did not see the danger in my situation. Reasons could be that God hates divorce; people just did not want to be involved in a breakup of a relationship.

Three weeks of hell were over and we were back in the United Kingdom and I began to plot my exit in secret. I had a timeline of 2 months to make it happen but it ended up happening in 3 weeks.

The first thing that happened with the kids was that, when we got back, the nursery had a meeting with me because my daughter was a totally different person. She was chattier and more social with the other kids. This had not happened in her four months of being there. In just 3 weeks living in a house full of people she broke loose. When I went to my son's school one of the teaching assistant greeted me with, *"Welcome back from America"* and I wondered how she knew about that. She said my son had told her everything, about his Grandma, his Grandpa, cousins and I was like *"Really?"* A boy that does not talk is now making efforts to express himself.

I mentioned the findings from school still hoping he would change a bit about getting the kids involved in more social activities but all fell on deaf ears...as usual! My son's school had a WhatsApp group SEN (Special Educational Needs), which I begged to be allowed on, however he monitored everything and would not let me access the physical activities for my son. Finally, the school suggested free music therapy for my son to help with his sensory needs and learning. It turned into a big argument that night, I just went from asking to do one thing to the other and listened to him say no to all, and in my head I kept saying, *"Yup, it's never going to change and it's time to go"*. But my decision came when he said, he could not let us leave the house without him accompanying us because we were being watched, and that he could see things and hear voices. It was not the first time I was hearing him say crazy things like that, he believed he was abducted by aliens and as a result when he was returned he could do unusual things, he could hear and see them. He once said, he was the one that killed the former President of Nigeria, General Sani Abacha, and he had done it in the spirit realm, he believed he controlled his clients, and could make them call him for jobs. He never believed Michael Jackson was dead and throughout 2018 he was happy when he found Michael Jackson on Facebook and had conference calls with him every Saturday morning. He believed Michael

Jackson appeared to him as a child and taught him how to dance. There were too many of such stories, which I took lightly over the years but this time I had new meanings and understanding to these things because all of the support services I had contacted, mentioned mental health and emphasized my unsafety. Everything I read online ended up with the victim being killed. It was that night I knew, that I had to leave instantly, death had been lingering around the house and I really needed to stop ignoring it and do something.

GREAT ESCAPE

I pretended everything was fine after the argument and the next day, while I worked from home, I activated my *Escape Plan.* I changed all my passwords for social media, bank, emails etc and then I sent an email that I could no longer continue with his requirements of me as a wife and if indeed he said I must comply then we need to take a break and ask ourselves what we are doing.

That simple email created a volcanic eruption from him and I started receiving phone calls from people saying, I shouldn't let him in when he got back. I wasn't sure what was going on but I locked all doors and windows. He came home at about 8p.m at night which was later than his usual, and was blowing hot and cold. I stayed indoors and watched and listened to him switch from one personality to other. Interestingly we had just watched "Bates Motel" the TV series and all I could think about was multiple personalities. He stayed outside from 8p.m until 1a.m in the peak of winter, banging on the door or pacing back and forth the street, until he finally left. In fear of the unknown, I sent this email to my family,

"Hello fam,

I'm sending this message to you all. Please in event that tonight doesn't go well and in event that anything should happen to me, please do not let (name off) gain access to my children as custodian. I believe and I'm convinced that he is mentally unstable and needs to get help.

The children will have a better life and future away from him.

I have asked him to come and pack his things in peace and stay away until we have come to an agreement and the way forward. Hopefully he complies.

Dot The following day he came back with a mediator and after over six hours of fruitless words, the mediator gave up. I remember the mediator trying to no avail to calm him down, constantly reminding him that the kids were present.

The mediator had brought him back into the house and intended to run off, and I insisted that I would ring the police on both of them. That was when the mediator, (A clergy and his client) put in more effort to remove him from the premises.

Back to my escape plan, as much as I would have loved to stay in that neighbourhood, keeping the kids in the same school, the house of course 90% of what was in it was purchased by me, I had to choose life. I imagined walking home from work and knocked on the head. I was way too informed on these matters to make that mistake. So I bailed with the clothes on my back and a few sentimental toys for the kids and our documents. Interestingly, when I handed the keys of the house to the neighbour, for him to collect, her remark was, *"I watched him last night, does he have mental health challenges? Please as you leave, don't ever look back."* She was the 7th person in the last 4 months that mentioned mental health.

While we all want to think the best of our beloved, when it comes to domestic abuse and escaping, you have to think of the worst case scenario to survive. Once you leave, never look back. I never did and here am, still alive after three years and counting being a voice to the voiceless!

Chapter 12

NEW LIFE

A fter leaving my abusive marriage, I did not know what to expect, I did not know how things would work but I hoped for co-parenting. I however gave up on the idea of co-parenting when it became clear that he wanted me and not the kids. I left an open channel for him to make arrangements to see the kids; but I also made it clear that he would not see me, just the kids. He did not make any arrangements to see them and the kids surprisingly never asked about him after we left.

I tried to give my children the life they never had, the opportunity to see and experience the world. They were 6 and 3 years old and there was a lot they had not done. They went to see the cinema for the first time, we went to a pantomime for the first time, and we went to the community centre. Soft play centres and trips to the playground like every other day. All of this was very new to us, and I recall how their faces would light up whenever I got back from work to say, *"Let's go to the playground"* To them it was like going to Disney Land.

Things I struggled with for years in my past life seemed to work out easily. For instance, bedtime that used to be a nightmare, the kids, especially my son would scream at night once you mention bedtime, they both would stay awake until midnight or later. However, after I left, 7p.m pretty much became bedtime. Once it was 7p.m at most 7.30p.m, they were snoozing. They were not grumpy about going to bed, they did not cry, they were happy to have a bed time routine. You see, these things never worked in our past life.

Within the first couple of months, the kids struggled with night terrors otherwise nightmares, they described monsters (interchanged the word monster with daddy) chasing them, screaming etc, they would jerk and turn in their sleep, sometimes sob in their sleep, but I stayed close and lavished them with hugs, cuddles and reassuring words. You see, traumatic events can also cause nightmares. If a child has experienced some type of traumatic event, they might have nightmares about it for several weeks or months afterwards. I was constantly, studying and empowering myself with knowledge because I needed to be ready for anything that might happen with the kids.

Unlike my past life where a lot of things were not allowed, I got them into child counseling which was amazing and the outcomes were both revelatory and alarming but not surprising. My kids were overly sensitive to bright lights like the sunlight, especially my daughter who could hardly open her eyes when we went out in the sun. The house was never well lit, curtains drawn and no sunlight. They hardly went out to play in the sun and now they struggled. I was advised by the doctors to give it time and get them sunglasses.

I registered my son in a new school and gave them a long speech about how he did not communicate much, how he would have accidents several times a day, could not socialize, and the school was amazing. Between Friday Afternoon and Monday morning when he started, they had built him a cubicle in class, with all his favorite super heroes, soft toys and sensory equipment. I also took extra clothing so they could change him. To my surprise when I got there to pick him up, I was told, he did not stay in the cubicle, he chose to sit with the other kids, that he had made some friends and had no accidents. They added also that he actually took himself to the toilet. I was gobsmacked. My son had never taken himself to the toilet in school in all two and half years of his schooling.

In the past four years of my children's life, we hardly ever had guests or visitors, just visits from my parents, my sister once a year and they were not used to it. So my saying things like, *"We are having guests, visitors, or my friends"* was a shocker to them. These words in fact were never in their vocabulary, I had to take time to explain a lot of things to them. They had an ice-lolly for the first time in their life;

they had no clue what it was. The first time I announced that they were going to a BBQ, they had no clue what it was too. Things like picnics only existed on YouTube. I introduced them gradually into these things, because I did not want to overload their system. They rode a bicycle and a scooter for the first time, went to a Pantomime, and the playhouse. Dealing with crowds and noise was a bit tasking for them, so I aimed for autism friendly events for both kids because my daughter was also exhibiting a lot of autistic traits, it became difficult to tell if she was on the ASD spectrum or just copying her brother. I took them to places like a library, dance classes where my son chose street dance and my daughter ballet. I registered them for swimming and other sporting activities, all of which were never allowed in their past life.

UNLEARNING ABUSE

One of the observations from the people we lodged with when we first left was that my kids were unusually quiet for their age. If they sat to watch TV, they would not ask to have the channel changed, they would not touch the remote, and they would sit still and not move. They did not communicate their needs. This was because they were terrified of being shouted at like in their past life for touching remotes, phones, TV screen, their dad's work table, the keyboard, just anything really.

They would not ask for anything except being offered. Now this was an issue for my son in school. Even if he was dehydrated, he would not speak, he had to wait until asked. My children could not communicate their care needs. I had to begin reassuring them that it was okay to ask for things, it was also okay to disagree and not agree with everything mummy said. I introduced choices, letting them make a choice of what they wanted to do or when they wanted to eat. We planned things as a family. I remember the first time I said, *"What shall we do this weekend?"* They both looked at me confused because all their lives, weekends were spent at home. They were introduced to things like, making a shopping list and then going into the shops to find them which were a sharp contrast to our past life where most shopping was done online, the only person allowed in an actual shop was him.

By Easter break, I registered the kids in a club, to allow me cope with work and that brought out more revelations. This club had a lot of male staff and my daughter was terrified of men. She would scream when any of them approached her. Another time, my son hit his sister with a toy on her head and the incident was unprovoked. I was called out of work on so many instances, due to issues with my kids and interacting with others. My son would sometimes have outbursts of rage, growling, I would just hug him and make him breathe and count with me. Initially, he did not like to be touched, hugged or cuddled, but after we left, he began to request hugs and cuddles, which was very heartwarming for me. I made my kids recite things, like, *"In this house, no screaming, shouting or hitting, only love, kisses and hugs."* It was interesting how over time the violent sides of them began to subside. It was different, because in our past life, whenever my son had an outburst his dad just says,

"Leave him, he's a boy or just give him whatever he wants to stop him from screaming." In our new life, they both recited words like,

"I do not get a reward for bad behaviour!"

My daughter displayed way too many signs of anxiety while my son was just numb in several areas of his emotions. I began to work on them. I read books, I took them for support meetings, and I joined communities. And like magic I began to see a lot of changes. For each stage I encountered, I was happy at the progress, but a lot of times I felt bad that I left them in such a chaotic house. I wish I knew better. My kids would freak out, or apologise, or even try to sort out spilled milk instantly, they would be shaking. I reassured them that it was okay to make a mess; in fact I had to leave the house messy sometimes, just so they could have a bit of normal. With time, they got comfortable, asking for things, food, a drink or getting stuff from the fridge or cupboard.

A friend saw my children six months after we left and exclaimed,

"My! Look how tall they are." And I said well,

"Domestic Violence causes stunted growth"

We both laughed but I was being serious. My kids meals were restricted but when we left, our choice of menus were endless. I introduced them to different kinds of foods and fruits they had never tasted; just to expand their sense of taste. I worked really hard on emotions and expressing themselves rather than suppressing them. Within two months of the Early Help Officer seeing my son, her remarks were,

"He seems like a different child, has he received any specialist help?" I said *"No we are just living an abuse free life".*

Her comments were welcoming because on her first visit to the house, he had run off, no eye contact, no interactions but on her second visit two weeks later, he welcomed her with a *"Hello",* made eye contact, engaged with her even went ahead to tell her a story about his toys and what he was doing.

TRANSFORMED KIDS

I know people praise me for the super mum that rescued her children, but I am much more proud of my kids and their resilience. They are my battery pack, they keep me in the game they make me see how much it was all worth it but sometimes I think they really did not need to go through all that, and that is why I wrote this book for you to see that you do not need to let your children stay within domestic violence, you need to save your children. In fact you do not even need to be pregnant in an abusive home, do not stay there, and do everything you can to give them a normal life just like I did. Every time I see them do and try new things, I'm like *"wow".* , but there's always that other side of me that hurts for the wasted past years that made them handicap. **Don't stay for your children, Leave for them** From about two and half years old, my son had started regressing, and by five years old my son's social and communication skills were assessed to be at the level of a two year old. He always needed a teaching assistant next to him at school play and events. There was an incident where he tried to strip himself naked on stage at a Christmas recitals. We were not able to attend some events in school because he needed to be managed; I could not attend with my daughter and was not allowed to get a nanny, so he stayed home. He did not understand emotions and also struggled to express the few he could access. You'd be lucky to get a yes or no out of him. While British Sign Language and Speech Language Therapy were employed in schools, also an Educational Psychologist, not much progress was recorded with regards to his speech. But he responded to music and singing and so I sang to him. He also loved reading and his memory was great so I let him read as many books as possible. I did not understand how he could read any and everything yet couldn't communicate but I let him read. He had absolutely no self-care skills and was unable to initiate conversations. However, after I took a decision to put my kids first before me, leaving an extremely toxic situation not because of me but because I believed Children are the future and deserve good vibes and a safe space without even realising how much impact this would have on the kids or what the future held.

This same child immediately we left never had any wee accidents in school, began to speak and express his emotions, the same child was assessed 6 months later and was reported that he was at the level of his age however 1 year above his peers in comprehension of Math & English. This same child: school attendance has been 100%, never been sick one day since January 2019 in comparison to school attendance of 60%. His communication and understanding within a year of leaving the abusive situation, was accessed and rated at his key stage level. The school discontinued with The Picture Exchange Communication System (PECS), and Sign language, because he began to express himself. He is happy to be hugged and held close. He says things like,

"I love you mummy, I miss you mummy, are you sad, you look happy, you look pretty."

All of this had never happened. He used to struggle to walk short distances of seven minutes to school, now confidently does fifty minutes uphill trails. It is funny when he tells me I have to get fit; he seems to forget that only a few years back I had to carry him even when his sister could walk. He wakes me up at 4a.m and he is all cleaned, brushed and ready for school, ALL BY HIMSELF. He cooks a little and makes his own breakfast, and packs his lunch. In the first year of our leaving he played a key role in the schools assembly as Neil Armstrong and later that year he had the longest speech in the Christmas nativity show, he was one of the wise men. He has successfully participated in mud runs, relay races, and other sporting activities. I thought swimming would be impossible because of his sensory needs, but he has learned to swim at basic level. He is able to attend school trips unlike before and without issues.

My son was frightened of loud buzzy sounds, like the hand dryer, hair clippers etc. Having a haircut was a struggle at barbers, going into public toilets was traumatic for my son. Once the auto sensor dryer came on he would let off a high pitched scream. He would fight with all his energy not to go into the toilets at restaurants. Interestingly, 2 weeks after we left the traumatic house, my son asked to have his hair cut, he has had a haircut every other month since January 2019 with no fears at all. Remember the hand dryers? Immediately we fled the abuse, he seemed to be alright to come into public toilets with a bit of caution about the sound of the dryer. I always reassured him and his little sister was very good at encouraging him to try it. It was exactly 3 months after we left that he used the hand dryer, I broke down in tears as he dried his little hands and it was even funnier when he put his head underneath it. My tears turned to laughter.

It brings tears to my eyes seeing how much a child changed in a few months to a year of fleeing abuse. The one that melts my heart is how talkative he is. I literally cannot shut him up. One day I had to ask,

"Son, why did you stop talking all those years?" I swear I did not expect the response I got. He responded,

"It was because I was afraid of the darkness in the house."

It was creepy because he told me the exact house that made him stop talking. I remember an incident in that house, my son loved to go into the bathroom then one day he went into the bathroom and screamed. I checked him, he wasn't hurt and there wasn't anything that could have scared him. After that day he never wanted to go into the bathroom, he was terrified of it. Now my ex was very big on consulting spiritual powers, clairvoyants, mystical things. I remember my daughter especially, always fighting in her sleep. I do not know whether these spiritual things are true or not, I am just happy to have my kids, living free and happy.

Interestingly, a lot of behavioural actions I connected to autism on the part of my son, actually stopped after we left that house. My son is autistic but has made significant progress in a very short time and continues to make even more progress on a daily basis and that is all the validation and assurance I will ever need.

My daughter started to regress as well from two and half years, she became scared of people, and picked up a lot of autistic traits from her brother, the only other human child she interacted with. She became extremely shy, anti-social and would not use her words in public. Post abuse, she too has become very chatty. Her nursery teacher remarked that when they first met her, she thought this child would be hard work based on her traumatic background but my daughter shocked them with speedy transformation. In fact, she became the teacher's pet, the one that read to other kids and got them to settle down. At 3 years old, her poem got published and she is consistently topping everything she is involved in. She had shed off a lot of aggression, and learned characters from my son. She is constantly developing and discovering herself. She used to be very timid and afraid to try things, always scared of being bellowed upon or failing at a task, but now she is more comfortable and reassured. I let her know that she is safe and mummy is not going to be mad at her. My kids are amazingly gifted, my son plays the drums and my daughter plays the Ukulele. They can both ride a bicycle, which took forever to master because they struggled with coordination skills, a scooter as well but we got there in the end. All of this would have never happened if we stayed in that abusive house.

YOU CAN DO IT

Every year, millions of people all over the world are victims of domestic violence. If you or someone you know is in a situation that is unsafe, please provide the type of help and support you or they may need. Domestic violence can be one of the most difficult types of situations to talk about and to escape from. Sadly, it can happen to anyone – women, men, children, between spouses and even friends. No one is immune to domestic violence; encourage them to seek the necessary support and resources to get yourself or the person you know out.

To all the victims and survivors of domestic violence please know that when it comes to abuse, you believe there's no way out but there is always help. There is always a way out and at any given moment you have the power to say this is not how the story is going to end. **Trauma may happen to you, but it can never define you.** Never judge yourself by what others did to you. I know that sometimes the shame is not the beatings, not the rape but it in the shaming and being asked to stand judgement. Be armed with this knowledge: people are going to talk and judge you regardless of what choices you make, so please choose you and let them talk anyway.

Breathe. This is just a chapter in your life and not your entire story. You will feel exhausted and drained; this is only because you are probably around a narcissist. They are difficult, needy, controlling, verbally and mentally abusive. They are like vampires and won't stop until they suck you dry. In order to break free, you will need to accept that the abuser is who they are and is incapable of love or a deep connection, your children are not as important to them as you think. You were never loved, you were an object to be used and abused, you were their helium to keep them afloat, and acceptance of this fact will set you free. Once you are awake, they cannot stand a chance against you. Do it for yourself, do it especially for your children. You can do this, and I am rooting for you.

ABOUT THE AUTHOR

As early as six years old, Dot IkwerreGirl Acheru (DiGa) envisaged growing up to be a fierce lawyer however she ended up studying Foreign Languages and Literatures, with a major in French.

She was recruited as a Linguist at her first job in 2000, in the office of Rtd General Anthony Ukpo (of blessed memories), then as a documents translator for Le Meridien Ogeyi place Hotels from French to English and stood as a liaison between the French and English teams.

She proceeded to function in varying capacities in the Oil and Gas sector in Port Harcourt Rivers State Nigeria and this nudged her career towards Management. She later relocated to the United Kingdom where she acquired a Masters of Arts in Management, in Middlesex University, London alongside several certifications in Project Management, PRINCE2, Business Analysis, ISO, ITIL and more. She also has a diploma in Theology from Cambridge University.

With her qualifications she became a high profile U.K. Certified Project Manager in the Public Sector, while working with charities like Watoto, Compassion UK, Crisis, and within the busy schedule. She released her first E.P. album in 2009 whose proceeds went towards supporting the aforementioned charities. Worthy of note are her skills as a multi-instrumentalist, singer, performer and producer. Unlike the average female, Dot is fierce and undeterred, though her marriage from 2011 culminated in abuse, her inner strength has preserved her sanity and unrelenting wits.

In the past 3 years of being free of abuse and fear, she has built Talk2Dot www.talk2dot.com which is a safe haven where women are taught all they need to know about Domestic Violence. Talk2Dot also signposts women to other Charities where they can find solace and more support. She also founded a Community Club that supports Black, Asian and Minority Ethnic (BAME) women in London and Greater London in a number of areas, www.yanapeople.com is funded by The National Lottery Fund, and other UK Boroughs and organisations.

DiGa (Dot IkwerreGirl Acheru) https://www.ikwerregirl.com/wegive is a branch of her ventures which in its four years of existence, is growing strong, supporting single mothers and widows in Nigeria with housing issues, rent, meals, groceries and financial assistance for business start-ups.

She is blessed with 2 amazing kids, her strength and her joy, her current driving force...the **SILENT WATCHERS.**

SYNOPSIS

It all started as a very warm friendship that eventually ended in marriage; once those dotted lines were signed, I was trapped and nothing on earth would have prepared me for the turmoil I was to experience.

My ex-spouse's subtle unveiling as an abuser who thrived on control and subjection, created a dark wanton aura in the home which I never understood as **Domestic Violence.**

This book is a non-chronological narrative which recounts the horrors of domestic violence/abuse and its adverse effects on children over and above the primary receiver: the partner. It proffers solutions on both how to cope when found in such situations, and how to eventually make a safe exit for the sake of the wellbeing of the children- **THE SILENT WATCHERS.**

Printed in Great Britain
by Amazon